IN LOVING MEMORY OF

KRISHNA SAHARIA DAS

FROM

SPRINGFIELD FRIENDS

INDIA

LIFE, MYTH, AND ART

INDIA

LIFE, MYTH, AND ART

CHAKRAVARTHI RAM-PRASAD

BARNES
& NOBLE
NEW YORK

India: Life, Myth, and Art

For Krishnan and Nalini

This 2007 edition published by Barnes & Noble, Inc., by arrangement with
Duncan Baird Publishers

Copyright © Duncan Baird Publishers 2006
Text copyright © Chakravarthi Ram-Prasad 2006
Commissioned artwork and map © Duncan Baird Publishers 2006
For copyright of photographs see page 144, which is to be regarded as an extension of this copyright

Editor: Diana Loxley
Managing Designer: Daniel Sturges
Managing Editor: Christopher Westhorp
Picture Researcher: Julia Ruxton
Commissioned artworks, decorative borders and map: Peter Visscher

ISBN-13: 978-0-7607-8951-3
ISBN-10: 0-7607-8951-7

Library of Congress Cataloging-in-Publication Data is available

Typeset in Perpetua and Truesdell Bold
Color reproduction by Scanhouse, Malaysia
Printed in Singapore by Imago

1 3 5 7 9 10 8 6 4 2

NOTE
The abbreviations BCE and CE are used throughout this book:
BCE Before the Common Era (the equivalent of BC)
CE Common Era (the equivalent of AD)

Photographs on preceding pages: Page 1 – A late 16th- or early 17th-century CE book cover of painted
wood, from Bengal, illustrating the Rasa mandala. Page 2 – Partial view of a columned shrine within
the Jain temple of Vimal Vashi at Mount Abu, built in 1032CE and dedicated to Adinath. Page 3 –
A Chola bronze figurine of the god Ganesha, from Tamil Nadu, 11th–12th century CE.

CONTENTS

IMAGE AND IMAGINATION

India is an ancient land of rich and vibrant contrasts, with a range of influence that has touched many parts of Asia, well beyond the borders of the modern nation-state of India. This vast country, with its diffuse boundaries (over mountains and through deserts and rivers), constantly interacted with other cultures, creating a civilization of staggering diversity. It gave birth to, or took in, most of the world's great religions, and continues to foster creative relations with them. Such diversity is apparent even within the country's dominant religion, Hinduism, which itself is the general name for a collection of highly pluralistic practices and beliefs. Thus, the myths of India are endless, its art manifold, its life inexhaustible. As is often claimed, everything and its opposite are true in this ancient land – what follows gestures toward this glorious profusion.

THE SOUL OF INDIA

RIGHT Brahma was known as the grandfather of the *devas* (gods). While seldom a major figure of worship, he was regularly depicted in temple carvings in a multi-headed form, as in this four-headed sandstone statue from the 10th century (although only three of the heads are visible here). In his capacity as the overseer of the formation of the cosmos in every new cycle of its existence, Brahma is sometimes also referred to as the creator god.

Unity and multiplicity are in constant interplay in Indian thought. In the oldest extant texts, the sacred *Veda*s (ca. 1500–1100BCE), an array of natural forces (including the wind, fire, sun, moon, rain and the dawn), as well as abstract concepts, such as speech and the mind, are personified as an endless number of deities, indicating the pervasive presence of divinity in all things. There are also an infinite number of worlds, each occupying different realms and inhabited by numerous objects and beings, from giant planets to tiny creatures. The lives of humans are embedded in this pluralistic reality. All these diverse entities are interlinked through their natures and their actions, contributing to the sustenance of a cosmic order, *rita* (Sanskrit, *rta*). It is the duty of the priests to re-create and maintain this cosmic order by means of ritual performance (according to instructions given in the *Veda*s).

At times, the *Veda*s seem to indicate that such order can be traced back to one supreme source or being. In the slightly later texts, the *Upanishad*s (1200–600BCE), this idea of a single, unifying source of all reality emerges more clearly. In some passages, the fundamental ground of consciousness, or *brahman,* appears to be a supreme, divine being who creates the world and is immanent in it, including in humans; in others, it is better understood as an impersonal principle of being, whose inexpressible yet universal existence explains everything else. In either case, the *Upanishad*s teach that the purpose of individual human existence is to leave behind the apparent multiplicity of ordinary reality and to attempt to realize the intimate presence of *brahman* in the self. As the *Rig Veda* declares: "Truth is one, although the wise speak of it in many ways."

The *Veda*s were originally composed for and confined to the priestly elite. However, the Buddha and Mahavira, the founders of Buddhism and Jainism respectively,

reacted to the esoteric teachings on ritual in the *Vedas* and sought to make the apprehension of reality accessible to all. They both claimed that reality was endlessly varied and that its variety carried with it suffering for creatures who existed within it; however, they differed on how freedom from such suffering could be achieved (see page 62). These lessons on suffering had a deep impact on subsequent Hindu thought. Many Hindu philosophers acknowledge that the world of multiplicity is a world of suffering, but that one should seek insight to free oneself from it. The sacred and authoritative *Bhagavad Gita* (see page 58) teaches that there are many different spiritual paths through life – of action, meditation, intellectual inquiry and pure love for the divine. Yet the goal of all these paths is the attainment of a state in which one sees oneself in all and all in oneself, in which the suffering brought about through an egotistic distinction between self and world is transcended.

Although the seers had arrived at an understanding of *brahman* as the ultimate and unifying being, popular beliefs still kept spreading into the worship of many forms of the divine. In particular, the gods Vishnu and Shiva became seen (from the fourth century BCE onward) as the supreme form of the divine, superseding the deities of the *Vedas*. Although many deities were accepted in myriad forms, Vishnu and Shiva became dominant and possessed their own pantheons, into which a large number of other gods were incorporated. The ancient cults of the Mother Goddess and the Earth Mother gradually coalesced into belief in the Devi, God-as-She; but even here, other feminine forms of the divine persisted (see pages 108–111).

Buddhism and Jainism, while rejecting the idea of God, nevertheless participated in this joyful proliferation of forms. Even monotheistic Islam, when it came to India between the eighth and eleventh centuries CE, interacted creatively with

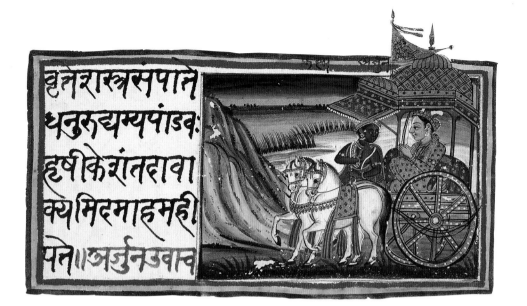

Hinduism to produce versions of Sufism in which many saints and endless songs mediated between the human and the divine. The diversity of life was also represented in the classical idea of the four human goals (*purushartha*s): ethical conduct (*dharma*), material prosperity (*artha*), pleasure (*kama*) and ultimate freedom or *moksha* (Sanskrit, *moksa*). While seeking to provide a single, over-arching theory of human life, the classical Indian thinkers nevertheless acknowledged that people will look for different things, and in different ways.

A thread that runs through the original Indian religious traditions is the presupposition that, rather than just one life and one afterlife, there is a long sequence of lives (*samsara*) until liberation (*moksha* or *nirvana*) is finally attained. What sustains this sequence is the seeding of consequences by every action (*karma*) one undertakes. If the consequences of an action are not met in this life, they require another life, and so on. Into each new life the individual brings the consequences of previous lives, and in experiencing them, creates consequences anew; only a proper life and true insight into the nature of action (and for many Hindus, only the grace of God) can bring freedom from new consequences.

ABOVE **This 19th-century manuscript painting represents one of the most famous scenes in Hindu narratives: Krishna (left), the divine incarnate, turns his head to instruct the warrior Arjuna on the meaning of life, action and faith. These teachings form the basis of the *Bhagavad Gita* ("The Song of the Blessed"), an episode within the epic poem known as the *Mahabharata* (see pages 56–59).**

UNITY FROM DUALITY

Among the most powerful representations in Hindu thought of the unity that is
believed to lie at the very heart of existence are the sacred symbols of the *linga* (the
symbolic phallus, above left and right) and the encircling *yoni* (the vagina and
womb, above left and right). The god Shiva is sometimes worshipped in the form of
the androgynous deity Ardhanarishvara (above), who is a synthesis of these male and
female principles. But he is most often worshipped through the *linga*, which
protrudes from the *yoni*. Together, the two symbols signify the union of male and
female and the totality of existence. Sexual love was accorded a respected place
within human life, as commemorated in the erotic friezes that adorn the walls of the
eleventh-century temple complex at Khajuraho, Madhya Pradesh (right).

THE STORY OF INDIA

The Indian subcontinent's first major civilization arose in about 2600BCE along the Indus River in what is now Pakistan. The two great cities of Harappa and Mohenjo Daro were home to some 30,000 people supported by agriculture. Each city had a citadel, communal granaries and streets of houses laid out in a grid pattern. There were elegantly engineered water supplies with covered brick sewers for waste, and builders used a fired brick that enabled them to repel floodwaters from the mighty Indus. The Harappan people traded with Mesopotamia and Egypt, and their artisans worked in copper, bronze, ivory and wood. They were the first culture known to have made cotton cloth. The Indus culture thrived for more than 600 years, but began to decline between 2000 and 1750 BCE – perhaps as a result of rising sea levels and the silting up of rivers, which would have damaged trade.

The connection between the culture of the Indus and the subsequent civilization that appears to have arisen by the middle of the second millennium BCE further east in the Indo-Gangetic plains is unclear. Archeological evidence unearthed from the Indus Valley sites indicates a flourishing culture that produced an abundance of material goods and artefacts. By contrast, all that is known of the later civilization is from the oral texts the *Veda*s that are its greatest expression (see pages 54–55). There is evidence from these texts of the use of war chariots and iron weapons, a reverence for the cow and a pantheon of nature deities. The people of the *Veda*s, often called the Aryans (from their self-description as *arya*, "the noble"), lived in clans under the rule of a warrior-chief (Sanskrit, *raja*). Priests performed *yajna* (sacrifice) to honour the gods, ensure prosperity and validate the chieftains' rule, and a system of social delineation was observed. The Aryans gradually turned from cattle herding to wheat farming and established the first Indian political entities,

BELOW **This Zebu bull is one of the most magnificent, and rare, examples of the seals produced by the Harappan culture (bulls are frequently found on pottery and other artwork, but seldom on seals). With its connotations of power, pride and virility, the bull motif is believed to have been one associated with influential officials. Although Harappan script remains undeciphered, it is by means of seals such as this that important insights have been gained into the culture's economic, artistic and elusive religious life.**

which combined dominant forms of kingship with republican participation by elites; monarchies, however, gradually came to prevail.

Another urban civilization developed along the river Ganges in the period 700 to 500 BCE. In the fifth century BCE the kings of Magadha, based at Rajagriha in the northeast, established themselves as the dominant power in the area. Wealthy trading towns at Kashi (modern Varanasi), Ayodhya and Shravasti had all the trappings of an urban economy, including coins, private property, guilds, banks and a common script known as Brahmi. The relative prosperity of these kingdoms facilitated the pursuit of philosophical ideas, while trade networks enabled the transmission of intellectual, commercial and other cultural influences across North India.

The most important political aspect of this period appears to have been a contest between the *kshatriya* class (warriors) and the previously pre-eminent *brahmins* (priests) over the significance of the latter's controlling knowledge of the sacred rituals. While this tension was usually resolved by creating an elaborate balance between the temporal power of the warrior-king and the ritual authority of the priest, some *kshatriya*s denied altogether the authority of the *brahmin*s over spiritual life. Foremost in this challenge were Siddhartha Gautama, or the Buddha ("Enlightened One"), and Vardhamana or Mahavira ("Great Hero"), the founder of Buddhism and the teacher of Jainism respectively (see pages 62–66). At this time, Buddhism and Jainism assumed equal importance. Buddhism was, however, eventually to have the greater impact in Asia, although its influence was largely limited to northeast India until the third century BCE when the first comprehensive Indian empire-builder, Ashoka Maurya, became an enthusiastic convert to the new religion, popularizing it and spreading its teachings far and wide (see page 20).

ABOVE **Cast as the Gupta Empire neared its zenith, during the reign of Chandra Gupta II, this early 5th-century CE gold coin (both sides of which are shown here) is of a type known as the "Lion-Slayer", embodying the Indian concept of a *chakravartin* (a "wheel-turner" or ideal ruler). The Gupta dynasty's period of rule witnessed several important artistic, intellectual and religious developments, which in combination mark the era out as the classical age of India (see pages 78–79).**

The period after Ashoka's death saw a revival of the power of the *brahmins*' religion. Devotional cults glorifying Shiva and Vishnu became increasingly popular. Additions to the epic poems the *Mahabharata* and the *Ramayana* (see pages 56–59) put growing emphasis on the divinity of their heroes Krishna and Rama, who were adopted as incarnations of Vishnu. In various mythic compositions known collectively as the *Purana*s (see page 56), Shiva and Vishnu in their many forms came to be given coherent narratives.

Apart from the rule of the Buddhist Kushanas, who created an empire extending from modern Afghanistan to northwestern India, there were only short-lived and unstable kingdoms until the Gupta dynasty emerged to forge a new empire in northern India in the fourth century CE (see pages 78–79). The rule of Chandra Gupta I (r.320–335CE) and his successors was a period of religious tolerance in which the key tenets of Hindu practices emerged.

South India was relatively isolated from the North, apart from a brief incursion by Samudra Gupta I. By the first century, there is literary evidence of a culturally advanced yet politically unsophisticated geographical area dominated by Tamil, the oldest Dravidian language, quite distinct from the Indo-European Sanskrit and its successors found elsewhere. Several overlapping peoples – the Pandya, Chera and Chola – appear to have co-existed, each styling their traditional land as a "kingdom".

Incursions by Huns from Mongolia helped to end Gupta rule. In the South, the Pallava, then the Rashtrakuta and finally the Chola dynasties dominated between the sixth and tenth centuries, sometimes using naval power to extend their influence to Southeast Asia and conquering swathes of North India. In this period, the religious, Sanskritic culture of the North influenced the South, creating a composite culture

RIGHT **This map shows the vast Indian subcontinent, together with its important topographical features and a selection of places, both modern and ancient (denoted by solid and outline dots respectively).**

HINDU KUSH

KIRTHAR RANGE

• Islamabad
• Jhelum

Chenab
• Amritsar

Jhelum
○ Harappa

▲ MOUNT KAILASA
• Badrinath

HIMALAYAS

Sutlej
Kurukshetra ○

Indus river

○ Mohenjo Daro

Ganges river

THAR DESERT
• Delhi
Mathura •
• Jaipur   • Agra
Chambal river

• Lucknow
• Ayodhya
Brahmaputra river

• Karachi

▲ MOUNT
ABU

Yamuna river
Varanasi • ○ Sarnath
○ Rajagriha
• Bodh Gaya

• Sanchi
Khajuraho •   • Bharhut
• Tigawa

• Dhaka

Dvaraka ○ • Shatrunjaya ○ Lothal
VINDHYA RANGE
Narmada river
SATPURA RANGE
• Nagpur

Kolkota [Calcutta] •

MOUNT GITNAR ▲

Mahanadi river

Tapti river
• Ajanta
• Ellora

Godavari river
Mumbai [Bombay] •
Elephanta Island

• Pune

• Nagpur

BAY OF BENGAL

ARABIAN SEA

DECCAN PLATEAU

Krishna river

• Hyderabad

• Badami

WESTERN GHATS

EASTERN GHATS

N
W   E
S

• Chennai [Madras]
• Bangalore
○ Mahabalipuram

Coleroon river

INDIA

SCALE   250 miles
├────────┤
0   400 km

• Tanjavur

ANAI MUDI ▲   • Madurai

INDIAN OCEAN

SRI LANKA

in which Shiva and Vishnu were adopted as southern deities, the languages of Telugu and Kannada developed out of a combination of Tamil and Sanskrit, and traditional southern temples took on classical northern layouts.

Traders had brought Islam peacefully to South India in its early years, but in 711CE, Arab forces led by Muhammad ibn Qasim conquered Sind (a region of modern-day Pakistan across the border from Rajasthan) and local peoples were converted to Islam. This province of the caliphate remained isolated until the early eleventh century, when the Afghan ruler Mahmud of Ghazni invaded India in the name of Islam. His campaigns laid the foundations for the success of others and in 1193 a formidable army of the Ghur caliphs conquered Delhi and began a period of Muslim ascendancy known as the Delhi Sultanate. Muhammad of Ghur's successor, Qutb ud-Din Aibak, erected a great tower, 240 feet (73m) in height, to celebrate the triumph of Islam in India (see illustration, page 84). The Sultanate reached its peak under Ala ud-Din Khilji in the early fourteenth century, extending far into and devastating the South before incursions by the Mongols forced the sultans to turn back northwards. Despite this consolidation, in 1398 Delhi was sacked and the Sultanate was reduced to one of a number of competing Muslim powers in northern India.

This period saw the establishment in the South of the last great Hindu kingdom, Vijayanagar (1336–1565), whose rulers sought to both establish continuity with the traditional southern Hindu dynasties and to innovate a public culture that accepted the novel presence of Islam within a Hindu framework. With the collapse of Vijayanagar, the southern Muslim sultanate of Bahmini came to dominate the region, until gradually much of the South also came under the sway of the Mughals.

Between the twelfth and seventeenth centuries, an influential form of public spirituality emerged across India that was centred on emotional devotionalism (*bhakti*) toward a personalized deity. It drew on older traditions and assimilated Islamic characterizations of God into Hindu discourse.

The next dynastic shift in India's fortunes occurred in 1526 when the Afghan leader Babur captured Delhi and founded the Mughal Empire. Under the rule of Akbar (r.1556–1605), India enjoyed one of its most successful and enlightened periods. Both his son, Jahangir, and his grandson, Shah Jahan, presided over an age of relative stability. Jahangir's killing of Guru Arjun was decisive in the creation of Sikhism as a separate religion. Shah Jahan was no less ruthless in his consolidation of power, although he was tolerant of Hinduism once his position was secure.

The rule of Shah Jahan's son, Aurangzeb (r.1658–1707), who destroyed Hindu temples and forcibly converted many non-Muslims, marks the decline of the empire at its geographical height. Numerous rebellions were ruthlessly suppressed. The Maratha people, under Shivaji (lived 1627–1680), attempted to provide a self-consciously Hindu challenge to Aurangzeb. After Aurangzeb, the Mughals became weakened by endemic factionalism and Delhi was eventually sacked in 1739 by the Persian Nadir Shah. But just as a new generation of indigenous powers began to emerge, India was to enter a new and decisive phase of its history, this time dominated by the growing involvement of European trading powers, notably the Dutch, French and British, the last of whom would seize control of much of this ancient land and unify it into the Raj.

BELOW Indian craftsmen were the pioneers of a distinctive style of intricate carving and inlay work in jade, as shown in this exquisite 18th-century green jade sword handle, inlaid with gold, from the Mughal Empire.

THE LEGACY OF ASHOKA

In the wake of his accession to power in ca. 268BCE, the Mauryan king Ashoka attempted a remarkable experiment in government. In 261BCE he embarked on the conquest of the lands on the east coast of India, now covered by the state of Orissa. The carnage affected him deeply and thereafter he adopted the teachings of the Buddha as his own, renouncing war and attempting to care paternally for his subjects. Throughout his realm he had edicts erected propagating mutual respect among his subjects and a standard ethic of personal and public conduct.

At Sanchi, Ashoka constructed eight *stupa*s – buildings designed to house bodily remains and other relics associated with the historical Buddha and his early followers – which took the form of a solid stone or brick dome with a top projection known as a *chatra* ("umbrella"). Depicted here (right) is the East gateway, or *torana*, at Sanchi, with the dome of the Great Stupa visible in the background. The three architraves of the gateway are decorated with solar spirals, winged lions, peacocks and *yaksha* fertility and power figures. From top to bottom, the central areas show: the previous *buddha*s, the Buddha leaving his palace at Kapilavastu and Ashoka visiting the Bodhi tree. The left post is missing its finial.

Ashoka's imperial edicts, carved on rocks and on sandstone pillars, promulgated *dharma*, a universal law for an extensive empire. At one time, it was thought that he used the edicts to promote his Buddhist faith. But more recently, given the use of the term *eusebeia* ("piety") in areas where Greek influence was strong, scholars have argued that he was primarily trying to create a culture of unity in diverse imperial lands that were home to many faiths. This had a religious element to it but was not narrowly Buddhist since the edicts urged respect for all spiritual beliefs and practices.

Ashoka's continuing significance is demonstrated by the fact that his imperial column has been adopted as the official symbol of the modern Indian state.

THE ART OF INDIA

The dominant Hindu conception of aesthetics comes from the *Natya Shastra*, ascribed to the sage Bharata (ca. 200BCE–200CE). It focuses on the nine main feelings experienced by humans: delight, laughter, sorrow, anger, energy, fear, disgust, wonder and tranquillity. These feelings are correlated in later literature with their own essence or flavour (*rasa*): the erotic, the comic, the compassionate, the furious, the heroic, the frightening, the hateful, the marvellous and the peaceful. A work of art – whether painting, sculpture, drama or dance – is lifeless if not infused with an essence. Each *rasa* is represented by a colour and a presiding deity: for example, the colour white and the god Shiva are assigned to the comic *rasa*.

In traditional Indian culture, artists do not so much express themselves as empty themselves. Creativity is not the product of an ego but the result of openness to divine inspiration. The art is the greater for the artist being only a conduit of aesthetic perfection. Accordingly, nothing is known of individual sculptors, dancers and architects, only of their artistic creation. Preparation and performance must follow established patterns, as the artist seeks to transcribe tradition perfectly. Instructions on invocatory rituals, proportions, gestures, expressions, rhythms, must all be rigorously adhered to. It is within the interstices of tradition – in the intricate, spontaneous interpretation of it – that novelty is found.

Classical dance of the style now known as *Bharata natyam* ("the dance of Bharata" – meaning either the eponymous author of the treatise on aesthetics or India itself by its traditional name) was initially performed only in temples by women. Today, however, it is a stage art. Preceded by religious invocation, the dance is divided into two parts: the abstract and the narrative. In the former, sets of technically precise movements create a geometric space and seek a pure appreciation of

symmetry; in the latter, a narrative is enacted through the use of recognizable expressions and gestures. At the same time, a combination of the two parts is also played out, skilfully joined to invoke a particular essence or sentiment (*rasa*) in the audience. The rigour of the discipline allows for considerable interpretive creativity.

A similarly strict set of procedures regulated the sculpting of religious icons. The sculptor was instructed to begin preparations only on a propitious day and to have the stone bathed in the urine of a breed of cow believed to symbolize the creative energy of the great Goddess. After bathing, meditating and making offerings the sculptor could begin work. Important aspects of body proportions, facial expressions and iconic features were all stipulated. Yet out of this discipline arose the multitude of sculptural forms that we recognize as Hindu. While granite was the main medium of ancient and classical sculpture, marble and soapstone also became

popular over time, especially through the influence of Jainism in eastern India; and after the Chola kings of South India (ca. 850–1279CE), bronze was often used in that region. Carving extended from monumental sculpture to exquisite work on ivory and sandalwood, on both religious and secular themes.

While adherence to traditional discipline is a feature of the classical art of India, there is much fluidity in styles and expressions. With sculptures, there is the practice of covering the walls and towers of temples, as well as the sides of the chariots in which icons were taken through towns, with an endless series of figures. Themes from well-known sacred narratives, both pan-Indian epics and local stories, dominate the carvings. But there are also individual friezes and units displaying activities that encompass all human, animal and vegetable life. Paintings are usually narratives and often focus on secular themes, such as hunting and courtly life.

The same tremendous diversity is evident in dance: some dance forms such as *Odissi* and *Kuchipudi* derive from the same classical roots as *Bharata natyam* (see pages 104–105), while others like *Kathakali* are strongly regional narrative dance-plays with their own internal rules on make-up, costumes and movements. Still other variations, such as *Kathak*, include classical elements but have little religious content because of their performance in Muslim and inter-religious settings. Numerous folk versions also exist throughout India, some confined to women or to men, some performed only for specific festivals, others common to whole groups and frequently danced. By their nature, these folk forms lack an identifiable history, but we can guess that their origins must lie deep in the Indian past.

The influence of Islam on India art is of equal significance. In Arabic culture, the proscription of any imagery of God, combined with the absence of illustrable

ABOVE **India's tremendous artistic heritage ranges from village crafts and simple carvings to the intricate bronzes of great temples; from traditional icons to more innovative designs that synthesize the influences of the country's different cultures. This delicate carved green jade reveals the Persian floral influence within Islamic Indian art in the Mughal period and beyond.**

narratives in the Quran, contributed to an Islamic interpretation that life forms could not be depicted. Persian art circumvented this by confining its representation to non-religious (political and natural) themes. This idea was followed by Indian Muslims, and by the Mughals in particular. Mughal painting was a creative fusion of Islamic interest in secular activity and Hindu use of symbolic imagery. After the Mughals, many regional styles of painting grew up in India into the modern period.

Another area of significant artistic activity was the production of jewellery: there is fascinating evidence from classical sculpture of the use of headdresses, necklaces, ear- and nose-rings, bracelets, anklets and belts. Among the oldest surviving examples of jewellery are ornaments on icons, some going back over a thousand years in Tamil temples such as Srirangam. Classical patterns such as the double-headed bird are still popular today. In North India, Islamic patterns interacted creatively with existing Hindu styles to create such spectacular gem- and gold-work as the incredible Mughal Peacock Throne, encrusted with diamonds, rubies, pearls and sapphires, that was carried away by Persian invaders in 1739 and subsequently destroyed.

Traditional Indian clothing consisted of various kinds of drapery, the most striking example of which is the sari – a long roll of cloth (up to 27ft/8.2m) worn by women, wound ingeniously around the waist and hung over the shoulder. Although saris are sometimes of basic cotton weave in a single colour and with little pattern, they can also ascend to heights of artistic expression, including complex silk weaves that incorporate pure gold thread (*zari* in Hindi, *jarigai* in Tamil) in organic and geometric designs. Weaves and designs are still associated with the traditional temple towns – Varanasi, Kanchipuram, Lepakshi – in which they are made.

BELOW **Carvings and statuary are important constitutive elements of temple architecture, and many of the large, famous temples are literally covered in them. But even more modest and simple structures often offer exquisite examples of the art, as in this delightful painted statue on the wall of a quiet temple in Mandi, Himachal Pradesh.**

THE SACRED IN STONE

ABOVE **A standing Buddha adorns the *stupa* within the 5th-century barrel-vaulted, rock-cut *chaitya* of Cave 19 (of 28 overall) at Ajanta in western India, hewn out by Buddhists between the 2nd century BCE and the 5th century CE. Some caves were created as residence halls and others for prayer and meditation.**

The oldest surviving architectural monuments in India are those erected by Buddhists; the previous thousand years of a civilization rich in literary creativity appears, puzzlingly, to have had no enduring buildings. The earliest architecture is found in the Lomas Rishi cave in the Barbar Hills, from the early third century BCE. The Maurya king Ashoka raised a celebrated pillar in the third century BCE marking his visit to Sarnath, the traditional site of the Buddha's first sermon. He also erected a commemorative pillar and eight *stupa*s (reliquary mounds) at Sanchi (see pages 20–21). Under his patronage and the rule of the Shunga kings of the second and first centuries BCE many commemorative shrines and *vihara*s, or monasteries, were constructed. The *vihara* consisted of residential rooms for monks built around a central courtyard. Under the Shungas, Buddhists developed the techniques of carving *vihara*s and excavated semicircular halls, *chaitya*s, from cliffs. Large sacred buildings made from wood were also erected in this era; they were multi-storied, with vaulted roofs and arched windows.

India's oldest surviving Hindu temples date from the period of the Gupta kings in the fourth to the sixth centuries CE, although in form they are derived from the Buddhist tradition. Cave-temples cut from the sandstone cliff at Udayagiri, Madhya Pradesh, included a shrine housing a Shiva *linga* (the phallic symbol of Shiva), a temple containing reliefs of Vishnu and Durga and another temple with a fine relief of Vishnu incarnated as Varaha (see page 100).

Hindu temples were initially built to a very simple design, with a square sanctuary behind a porch set with columns; after approximately 600CE they took the form of a more complex sanctuary set on a rectangular platform. From the fifth century onward Hindu temple architecture flourished, supported particularly by

RIGHT **Two of the earliest Hindu rock temples in South India from a group of five unfinished 7th-century structures at Mahabalipuram known as the *pancha rathas* ("five chariots", meaning vehicles of the gods). Shown here are the Arjuna Ratha (left) and the Bhima Ratha (right), created for the Pallava dynasty. Each is an imitation of Buddhist buildings of that time and wooden temples of an earlier period but they also set out the architectural elements of temple-building in South India for the following millennia with palatial columned pavilions and porches, sculpted pilasters, pyramidal towers and roofs, and an exuberance of decorative elements and constantly reinterpreted motifs.**

BELOW The Chalukya kings, who flourished between the 5th and the 7th centuries at Badami, Karnataka, were mainly followers of the god Vishnu, although they were tolerant of other Hindu and Buddhist sects. These 5th-century carvings are found in Cave 3, one of four huge pillared halls in a cliff overlooking Badami, and they show an iconographic depiction of Vishnu, which involves the *avatar* Vamana and is known as Trivikrama.

the Pratihara and Gupta kings in North India and by the Chalukya and Pallava monarchs in the South. Many forms, such as window shapes, appear to have survived from their wooden and thatched predecessors, but other elements, including increasingly tall towers, benefited from the use of hardier materials. Nevertheless, temple-building remained conservative, depending on techniques like post-and-beam and corbelled vaulting.

There are three major styles of temple architecture: the Nagara of the North, the Dravida of the South and the Vesara or Hybrid style of central India. The first is very varied because of its geographic range, but is generally marked by a curving tower surmounted by a cushion-like pinnacle. The second, more homogeneous style is recognizable through its pyramidal towers of rectangular cross-section. The third combines these and other features. In all of them, the outer parts of the temples contained a wealth of decorative and sacred carving – myriad images of deities, semi-divine figures and animals in the form of statues in recesses and of carved narrative tableaux depicting scenes of the gods and goddesses from myth.

Although the South Indian temples continued to be built in the same manner into the modern period, the North saw a transformation with the coming of Islam. Many major temples were permanently destroyed by invading Muslim armies. Few notable Hindu temples were built in the North thereafter, although several existing ones maintained their continuity, often with the support of local Muslim rulers.

Some Islamic buildings of the Delhi Sultanate, like the Adhai-Din-Ka Jhompra in Ajmer, were raised on destroyed Jain and Hindu monuments. But at the heart of the Sultanate, in Delhi itself, buildings such as the Quwat-ul-Islam mosque (1196) arose that spoke of early attempts to transplant Islamic architecture on Indian soil.

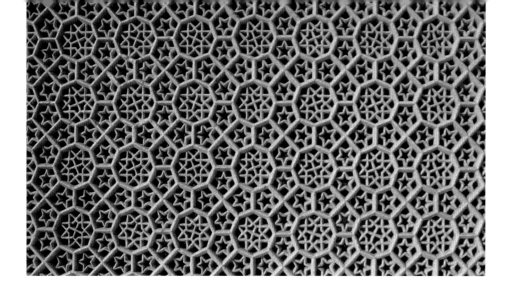

The key visual and structural elements introduced were the arch and the dome; but, of course, the functional differences between Hindu temples and Muslim mosques (*masjid* in Urdu) made for different layouts: the daily congregational nature of Muslim worship led to an emphasis on the central courtyard (*sahn* in Arabic) for worship, while the absence of images meant that the inner sanctum (the womb-house or *garbhagriha*) found in Hindu temples did not exist.

For Hindus, death was simply the passing of the body; for Muslims, the body awaited eventual awakening for passage into paradise. The Muslim kings and nobles therefore introduced a new form into Indian architecture: the mausoleum. This structure started out with the basic and unadorned geometry of cube and hemisphere in early Indian Islam and culminated in the Taj Mahal (see pages 90–91).

In the period of Akbar especially (lived 1543–1605, see page 19), but also of his immediate successors, Indian architecture saw an extraordinary fusion between Islamic and Hindu vocabularies, leading to an authentic new Indian style (known as Indo-Saracenic or Indo-Islamic). The most powerful creative expression of this style was in the new city Akbar built called Fatehpur Sikri. Using Hindu and Muslim craftsmen from across India, it was designed to house Muslim Persian and Hindu Rajput nobles and their families, and served as the meeting place of Akbar's vast empire. Its greatest impact lay in the inspiration it provided for both an architecture and a cultural vision of India in which Hinduism and Islam fused in harmony.

ABOVE **As a result of the faith's strict interpretation of its scripture, Islamic art developed motifs derived from calligraphy and geometry to present a rich and infinite palate of intricately interconnected decorative designs which reflect Islam's belief in the sublime underlying unity of creation. This delicately carved perforated marble screen encloses the 16th-century tomb of Sheikh Salim Chishti within the Friday Mosque complex at Fatehpur Sikri.**

SANCTUARIES OF THE FORDBUILDERS

Ranakpur, which lies on the curve of a boulder-strewn river deep in the forested Aravalli hills in the southwest of Rajhasthan, is one of the largest and most exquisite Jain temples in India, financed by wealthy Jain merchants. The sunlight plays dramatically on its profusion of finely carved white marble, not least on the 1,444 spectacular detailed columns. A view of several such columns and of a magnificent corbelled dome, one of dozens within the complex, is shown here (right).

Built in the fifteenth century – mainly during the reign of Rana Kumbha of Malghad and under the supervision of his minister Dharanashah – the temple is dedicated primarily to Adinath, one of the *tirthankara*s ("fordbuilders"), ancient teachers of Jainism, whose guidance was believed to deliver people from the world of suffering to liberation. The main chamber, accessible through four entrances set to the compass points, contains four marble images of Adinath, whose symbol is the bull – the temple is therefore also known as the temple of the Four-Faced (Chaturmukha) Lord of the Bull (Rishabhadeva). In a corridor that surrounds the central chamber are elaborately carved porticos containing images of all twenty-four *tirthankara*s. Each portico is surmounted by a pinnacle bearing bells that provide a pleasing counterpoint to the two massive bells housed in the main chamber. Although Ranakpur fell into neglect in the seventeenth century, it has been restored over the course of the past hundred years.

THE INDIAN WORLD

LEFT There were powerful associations between nature and divinity in Indian thought, a belief that the sacred was manifest in the wind, the sun, mountains, rivers, rainclouds, trees and flowering plants. This spectacular detail from the Taj Mahal (see pages 90–91) exemplifies this reverence for nature as well as the Islamic love of patterns. The Mughals were enthusiastic adopters of the Italian technique of inlaying precious stones, known as *pietra dura*. Colourful agate, coral, cornelian, lapis lazuli, turquoise and other stones were used to depict a variety of flowers, with the results flowing so smoothly across the surface that they appear more like paintings than stonework.

From the earliest times, Indian civilization gained great insights into the world's most fundamental philosophical issues, such as the nature of time, the origins of the universe and the place of humans within it. Elaborate myths evolved with which people could easily identify and which both explained and gave symbolic expression to these complex questions. But alongside these narrative and intellectual traditions there was a vigorous engagement with the outside world, most evident in ritual. The discipline of yoga also developed as part of the individual's pursuit of spiritual progress. Such deep involvement with the many different material and spiritual dimensions of existence extended to a close relationship with the landscape, flora and fauna of India, all of which were considered sacred.

BELOW An illustration from a 17th-century manuscript showing a yoga posture, or *asana*, being held by a practitioner. Disciplined, and often painful, exercises such as this were designed to bring mind and body into a state of equilibrium and tranquillity to achieve a state of ultimate freedom.

CREATION

BELOW An important concept in Hindu belief is of the world arising out of, yet at the same time being contained within, a creator-god. A key moment in the sacred Hindu poem the *Bhagavad Gita* (see page 58), has Krishna, the heroic charioteer of Prince Arjuna, revealing himself as the Supreme Being and presenting His Universal Form (*vishvarupa*) – a theologically complex idea that is represented in this 18th-century Rajasthani miniature painting.

Like many cultures, the Vedic and Hindu traditions were consumed by the mystery of existence. Several of their texts offered metaphorical accounts of the origins of the universe. There are two such symbolic re-enactments of creation in the narratives of the *Veda*s: one takes the form of procreation, the other of sacrifice.

In one account, the universe was said to have always existed in a mysterious way as the spirit of the universal man, Purusha, who came into being only when he became self-conscious and declared "I am". He had the shape of a man and, looking around, felt the sensation of being entirely alone. Purusha longed for a partner – his desire brought a wife into existence and from their union the first humans were born. But since this union was incestuous, she was ashamed, and fled. As she ran, she was transformed into a succession of animals; but each time she changed, Purusha assumed the same form as her, and made love to her. This process continued until the many species of animal life, right down to the ants, had been created.

The other, distinctly Hindu, metaphor for creation is sacrifice. In one version, creation is the ritual death of the same primordial man, Purusha, who was said to have had a thousand heads, a thousand eyes, and a thousand feet. From his body emerged the gods and wise men, who then carried out an act that resembled the later brahminic ritual of casting oil, grain and clarified butter into the sacred flames. The butter they threw into the firepit was the season of spring, the fuel that flared up in the flames was summer, while the sacrificial act itself was autumn. The gods and sages then dismembered Purusha, creating the Earth from his feet, the air from his navel and the overarching sky from his head. The sun was his eyes, his breath was the wind god Vayu, and from his mouth issued the sky god Indra, and Agni, lord of fire (see page 36).

From the Gupta era (320CE) onward, temples were seen as miniatures of the cosmos and consequently were laid out on the plan of a giant Purusha, with the most sacred part established at his navel — the *garbhagriha* (womb-house), which contained the image of the temple deity. The medium of sacrifice, fire, was venerated as a symbol of *tapas*, a word that referred both to the power generated by sages through meditation and to the concentrated divine desire that manifested itself as creative energy.

The sages of the *Upanishads* spelled out the symbolic meaning of the creation narratives — sacrifice was to be understood as renouncing the sense of self and becoming universally free, thus attaining the status of the creator. A person who renounced the desire for personal gain and reward could even escape the law of *karma* (consequences of past actions) that would otherwise entangle him or her in the material universe and in *samsara* (the cycle of death and rebirth; see page 11).

Later Hindu theologians replaced mythic narratives with the actions of a supreme divinity and argued for more abstract conceptions of creation. Ramanuja (ca.1017–ca.1137) claimed that the world is the body of God: God, as supreme consciousness, self-creates the material world and is present throughout, just as consciousness is aware of its embodied self. Madhva (1238–1317) argued that God was so pure that the impure world of matter must always be something distinct. For him, God took eternally pre-existing matter and shaped it into the world; He is thus the controller but not the creator of the world.

The idea that some original matter pre-exists, already indicated in the early Hindu myths, was emphatically expounded by both Buddhism and Jainism: for these faiths, not only original matter but the world around us has always existed. We can only seek to become free of its ties.

FIRE AND TRANSFORMATION

In Indian religious ritual, the properties of fire were held to be sacred: in the act of cremation, flames, representing the forces of creation and transformation, offered up the human body and marked the departure of its *prana* (life-force) in death. The Hindu god of fire is Agni (above), who acts as a messenger between worshippers and the gods and is often depicted with two heads. Another deity associated with the light and warmth of fire is Surya, the sun (above, left and right), who is important from early in the Vedic period onwards. But perhaps the most enduring image is Shiva as Nataraja ("lord of the dance", shown in the twelfth-century bronze, right). His divine dance was believed to create, maintain and ultimately dissolve the universe, as represented by the girdle of fire that encircles him.

THE CYCLICAL COSMOS

Indian cosmology has myriad accounts of the origins of the universe. What unites many of these highly variable versions is the belief that the universe has been through numerous manifestations, that creation will be followed by disintegration and that both are part of an immense cycle. In short, time is inconceivably vast, and it is cyclical.

The standard metaphor for the enormity of time was the "day of Brahma", the creator-god. Each day of his life was equivalent to 8,640 million years on Earth. In the morning Brahma created the universe, then in the evening after a period called a *kalpa*, lasting 4,320 million years, he allowed order to collapse and chaos resumed. By night he rested, and his sleep lasted for another 4,320 million Earth years. Then a new dawn touched the sky and creation began once more with a new *kalpa*.

The *kalpa* of Brahma was split into 1,000 *mahayuga*s ("great ages"), each of which contained four *yuga*s ("ages"). Age by age, the spiritual quality of life gradually declined. Each era was associated with a particular colour. The first era was the Kritayuga, a perfect age lasting 1,728,000 years. All people in this epoch were

LEFT A horse-headed Kalki statue from North India, 19th century. The popular iconography for Kalki varies and includes a horse, a rider on a white horse, or a horse-headed person. As the final *avatar* of Vishnu, he has yet to make his appearance during the current cycle of time. His inevitable appearance will augur the end of our present age, which has led some to invoke him as protection from the effects of the re-creating process to come.

great sages. There was no work, for humans were not entangled by worldly desires, no fearfulness or hatred, no religious rites, no self-regard or disease. Brahma was white in this age. The Tretayuga lasted 1,296,000 years. Virtue had declined by a quarter. Humans lost their conviction of their unity in universal consciousness and began to use sacrifices and other rites in order to re-attain some lost state. Brahma was red in this age. People began to compete and were sometimes drawn into conflict. The third age was the Dvaparayuga; virtue had declined by half. Lasting 864,000 years, this age was marked by increasing human misfortune and the first appearance of disease. Humankind was driven more and more by selfish desire, some were dishonest. Brahma was now yellow. The Kaliyuga, lasting 432,000 years, is the current age of the world, in which virtue has fallen away by three-quarters. Political rule is through force. People suffer from diseases and natural disasters, and have been driven to live in teeming cities. Brahma has a black aspect.

But this cycle will end and another will begin. The end will not be a punitive destruction of the world, but an ordained stage in time. Different theologies tie the ending of each cycle to their conception of God. For followers of Vishnu, he will come as Kalki, the final *avatar* in the form of a warrior on a white horse who will usher in the end of this age. Another vision has him as baby Krishna, lying on a white basil leaf, sucking his toe in the pristine concentration of the infant, waiting to come out of his reverie and re-create the world. Kalki's name derives from the word for dirt, *kalka*, which denotes him as the "destroyer of foulness". For devotees of Shiva, it is his cosmic dance that spells both the birth and the death of the world, coming in a full circle through his dynamic movement; between cycles, he sits in ascetic meditation, suspending all time, space and matter.

THE BLESSED MOUNTAIN

In many of the world's cosmologies, mountains were afforded a particularly special status. In India, even simple hills could become sacred through the stories that were attached to them. In the Tamil country, for example, several hills are linked to tales of Murugan, the Tamil boy-god who became identified as the son of Shiva (see page 107). Yet India is a land containing more than mere hills; its northernmost areas are bounded by some of the greatest mountain ranges on Earth. One particular peak laden with spiritual meaning lies well beyond traditional Indian terrain – Mount Kailasa, the home of Shiva and his divine family. Contributing to its spiritual allure were the difficulties of access associated with its remote location in the mystical landscape of the mighty Himalayas (shown here, right, at sunset), one which recurs in many significant narratives: it is where the heroic Pandava brothers retire at the end of the epic *Mahabharata*, on their way to heaven; and Hanuman the monkey-god lives there as an immortal.

As the closest point on Earth to the heavens, mountains were often believed to be at the very centre of the world, creating a link between humans and the gods. According to one Vedic story, Brahma fashioned the Earth in the form of seven circular continents. The innermost one lay in a salt sea, its land rising majestically to the awe-inspiring Mount Meru, the centre of the universe; Bharatavarsa (what is now India) stretched out to the south. Seven layers of hell descended below the surface of the Earth, while seven layers of heaven rose above, culminating in the home of perfected spirits. From the underworld realm of the dead there stretched two paths: one for those who had achieved liberation from rebirth, following the northern path of the sun to the home of perfection; the other taking the sun's southern path to Earth, where souls weighed down with *karma* (consequences of past actions) were reborn. Both Buddhist and Jain cosmologies were influenced by these Vedic ideas.

SACRED GEOGRAPHY

In all of India's most sacred texts – including the *Rig Veda* (1500BCE), the *Upan-ishads* (1200–600BCE) and the *Bhagavad Gita* (first century BCE) – there is strong evidence to suggest that the ancient cultures felt an intense connection to the world around them. In some cases, the natural forces were personified as deities (*deva*s): rain, thunder, fire, sun, moon and the dawn. Nature could be powerful and frightening if humans distanced themselves from it, but properly understood and through correctly performed ritual it was possible to attain power over the secrets of nature, acquire immortality and make the world safe.

Within this generalized sense of an innately sacred world, there also developed the more specific idea of the landscape of Bharatavarsa (the Indian country) as

LEFT **In Mahabalipuram, 7th-century sculptors have adorned a rocky hill with the story of how the waters of the Ganges, which once ran only in the heavens, issued from Vishnu's toe. The Ganges is represented by the natural cleft in the rock, adorned with *naga*s, which would once have had water poured down it to simulate a waterfall. On one side (left) are the elements of the tale, while on the other (right) are scenes from the natural and celestial worlds. According to the myth, the sage Bhargava (in the yoga posture, above the shrine) sought to bring the Ganges down to Earth in order to wash away the impurities of his ancestors; his prayer was answered by the god Shiva (who holds a weapon, at Bhargava's right side).**

imbued with spiritual meaning. Special reverence was reserved for rivers. India's greatest sacred rivers – the Ganga (Ganges), Yamuna, and Sarasvati – were each associated with a goddess. The holiest is the Ganges, which supplies the subcontinent with its most potent spiritual symbol (see page 112).

Yamuna was the daughter of the sun god Surya and sister of the lord of the dead, Yama – for this reason, people who bathed in the Yamuna were said to lose their fear of death. The holy river was also sanctified by Krishna: as a baby he fell into it as he was being carried across by his father, Vasudeva, and his touch blessed its waters ever after. It is a matter of dispute as to whether the Sarasvati (named after the patroness of poetry, music and other arts) was a real river that has now disappeared or whether it was always a myth. Rivers – especially holy sites on them (such as Varanasi on the Ganges and Srirangam on the Kaveri) – contained *tirtha*s, places where the gap between the physical and spiritual worlds was forded. To be present there during festivals allowed one to attain a keener awareness of the divine. Mountains and hills were also laden with sacred significance (see page 40).

Forests were traditionally treated with cautious respect. While they were places of lost souls, demons and magical beasts, they were also home to great sages and their hermitages. Woods and groves retained the idyllic appeal of the forests, but without their perils. Even individual trees – and sometimes stones too – could be invested with spiritual power. A tree in the courtyard of a local temple would become the abode of a benign spirit and would often be hung with small cradles by those wanting a child. Mysteriously, a stone would speak of the presence of a powerful cobra – the snake that winds in watchful wonder around Shiva's neck – and the people would offer passing worship, incorporating its potency into their daily lives.

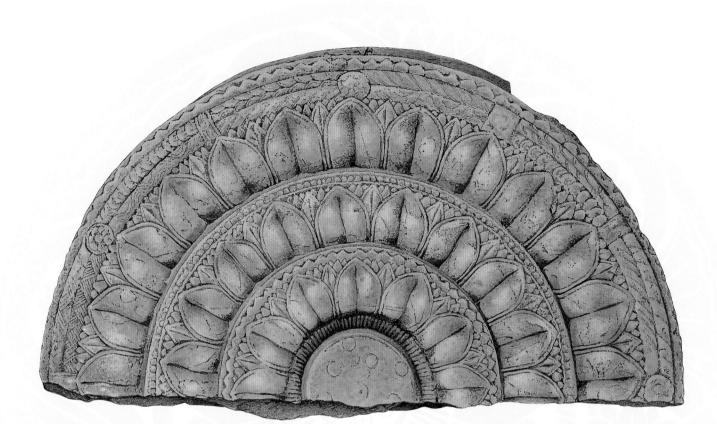

THE LOTUS OF PERFECTION

Indian art and sculpture attest to a deep reverence for the natural world. Among the most celebrated of images is the lotus flower (above, centre, right and left), a symbol of Earth's richness, fertility and beauty. In nature, the plant takes root at the bottom of a pond and sends up a thin white stalk toward the surface, where it blooms. Similarly, in one creation myth, the lotus stalk is said to rise from Vishnu's navel and to blossom in the form of a red flower bearing the creator-god Brahma. The word for "lotus" in Sanskrit is *aravinda* or *padma*: one of Vishnu's many names was Padmanabha ("lotus-navel"); his wife Lakshmi was also called Padma or Nalini (both meaning "lotus") – and the divine couple were a popular subject for painters, as shown here (opposite) in this 18th-century miniature painting.

REVERED CREATURES

The multiplicity of divine forms and the sense of the divine as immanent in nature combined neatly in the Hindu tradition of associating animals symbolically with the gods. Rudra, for example, a god of the cattle-herding Aryans, was envisaged as a fierce man mounted on a bull. This powerful deity, lord of cattle and storms, physician to the gods, and keeper of healing plants, was feared for his aggression and loved as a destroyer of wrongdoers and vanquisher of disease. He was given the epithet Shiva ("auspicious") and was later transformed under that name into a major form of the divine. Shiva retained his association with the bull, and was often represented with the bull Nandi, his attendant and mount. In every temple to Shiva a bull is situated facing the main sanctuary, gazing adoringly toward the inner sanctum. Nandi was as white as snow, with distinctive red horns. When represented as a man with a bull's head, he was referred to as Nandikeshvara, revered in myth as a teacher of music and dancing.

Cows were a particularly precious resource of the Vedic people. Wealth was calculated by the number of cows owned, and many a battle must have been fought over the ownership of herds – the Indian Aryan word for war was *gavisti*, literally "a looking for cows". The cow became associated with the earth and fertility – the earth goddess Prithivi, hymned in the *Rig Veda*, was sometimes represented as a cow and the animal was linked with the ancient cult of the universal mother. Her produce – milk, clarified butter and yogurt – was honoured by the ancients and used as cleansing agents as well as for nourishment.

Other deities were associated with animal attendants or mounts. Brahma, for example, was carried on a wild goose. Sarasvati, his consort and the sweet-tongued goddess of the arts was often

LEFT Depicted as an elegant figure in this 18th-century bronze statue from Madras, Hanuman the monkey-god, messenger and servant of the divine hero Rama, is said in the *Mahabharata* to have been golden-bodied with a ruby-red face and an enormous roar – the embodiment of power, humility, bravery and faithfulness.

attended by a white swan. Vishnu and his consort Lakshmi were carried by Garuda, half-giant and half-eagle, who was renowned for his courage. Garuda was usually gold-coloured with an eagle's head, human arms, feathered wings and a powerful round belly. Rama, one of Vishnu's earthly, descended forms (*avatars*), was assisted by Hanuman, his monkey attendant; Hanuman is the perfect devotee, and the young men who worshipped him often dressed up as monkeys to replicate in themselves his loyalty to Rama.

Shiva's and Parvati's elder son was the elephant-headed Ganesha, lord of beginnings, guardian of thresholds and the scribe to whom Vyasa dictated the great *Mahabharata* epic (see pages 56–58). Ganesha's attendant was a tiny mouse. His younger brother was Karttikeya (the Tamil Murugan), god of war, who rode a peacock. In a race around the world, Karttikeya/Murugan set off on his peacock, which he reckoned was faster than his big brother's small mouse; but Ganesha, recognizing this, cleverly argued that since his parents were the world to him and everyone else, he only had to go around them to win!

The snake was also regarded with awe. Vasuki was king of the *naga*s, serpent inhabitants of the underworld who combined a human head and torso with a serpentine tail. Their mythology developed from fertility cults in which snakes were worshipped. In one important myth, the gods and demons used Vasuki as a rope when they churned the cosmic ocean to create the sun and moon and extract the nectar of immortality (*amrita*). Both Vishnu and Shiva have associations with serpents. A hooded cobra is coiled obediently around Shiva's neck, indicative of the divine mastery of poisonous fear. In a very different metaphor, Vishnu reclines on a thousand-headed python, Shesha, whose coils embody eternity.

THIS WORLD AND BEYOND

By the third century BCE, a tension had emerged in the objectives of Hindu religious thought: on the one hand, there was a concern to live an ethical but socially engaged and prosperous life, and, on the other, to transcend the material world and, through asceticism, self-discipline and intellectual inquiry, attain a mystical state of being in which there was a unity of consciousness between self and reality.

These opposing views of existence were also evident in Buddhism. The dominant value was, of course, that of an ethical and responsible life with all its proper material trappings. This was the value of the householder, committed to work, family and community. The radical challenge to this was the spiritual route of a life spent in pursuit of insight into reality. This was the value of the renouncer: the one who gave up all thought of marriage, family, work and social labour and wandered the world alone or kept only the company of like-minded practitioners of spiritual discipline. But how were these two opposing values to be reconciled?

Early in its history (around the fourth to the third centuries BCE), Buddhism devised a solution to this problem (later replicated independently in Christianity): those who renounced the world to seek enlightenment could gather together in self-regulating communities of spiritual seekers, subjecting themselves to collective discipline. In return for using their spiritual power to bless and guide ordinary people in society, they would be economically supported by the latter. The monasteries and nunneries of Buddhism were the result of this compromise.

Hindu traditions did not adopt the idea of monastic orders until much later, but they did accept an account of the proper life, in which both values were accepted. The influential texts on social order and good conduct, the *Dharma Shastras* (fourth to first centuries BCE), suggested that there were four legitimate human goals,

RIGHT Between the 1st century BCE and the 5th century CE parts of Kashmir – including Harwan in the Srinagar Valley, where the tile (4th–5th century CE) shown here is from – were under the influence of Buddhism. In the top register, the tile's stamped decorations depict human profiles, and in the bottom register a series of geese – both were common motifs of tiles such as this (the goose represented the soul's yearning for release from *samsara*). The crouching figures in the centre are believed to represent ascetics – beings who would have renounced the material concerns of the world and lived a life of self-discipline, meditation and sustained intellectual inquiry in the pursuit of spiritual liberation.

grouped into two categories: ethical conduct (*dharma*), prosperity (*artha*) and pleasure (*kama*) on the one hand, and spiritual liberation or *moksha* (Sanskrit, *moksa*) on the other. Since these goals could not all be sought at the same time, a person could pursue the two categories at different times in his or her life. As a student, he would learn the sacred texts in preparation for life. Then, as a householder, he would marry, have children, work, bring prosperity to his dependants, and maintain the ritual fire and all the activities associated with it. Most people would spend the rest of their lives in this way. Others, however, would go on to a transitional life after their children had grown up: the retired married couple would become forest-dwellers, maintaining contact with society but also pondering on the ultimate questions. Again, many would end their lives in this stage. But for others, there would be a further stage. The renouncer would cut all ties with society and wander through town and forest, performing mental and physical austerities while seeking to gain spiritual awareness.

Conventionally, these stages of life would apply only to upper-class males from priestly (*brahmin*), warrior (*kshatriya*) or mercantile (*vaisya*) backgrounds, and not to either the labouring class (*sudra*) or to women. But several texts recognize both the right and the reality of all to renounce society for the sake of spiritual knowledge; and there are many stories of women and lower-class men becoming great teachers and spiritual savants.

THE PURPOSE OF PLEASURE

The civilization that explored the most ascetic and rigorous denial of the world in search of supreme truths also gave us a rich and natural account of life in the here and now. The most famous indication of this embrace of life is the *Kama Sutra*, a text attributed to Vatsyayana, from around the first century BCE. Although the ancient manual is perhaps best known for its cataloguing of sexual positions, this theme in fact constitutes around just one-fifth of its overall length; the majority of the text focuses more generally on the relationships between men and women.

The society in which the *Kama Sutra* was written was dominated by upper-class males and its intended reader was the cultivated man-about-town. Nevertheless, the book is strikingly open and nuanced in its approach to the problems of conduct

RIGHT A couple is shown amorously entwined in an 18th-century illustration, "Before Lovemaking", for the 16th-century text *Rasamanjari* by Bhanudatta. Among its other preoccupations, this text sought to categorize lovers according to experience, age and physical and emotional characteristics.

between the sexes. While appearing to guide men through their approach to women, it delineates the subtle and shifting emotions that mark relationships. It clearly acknowledges the initiative and autonomy of women; indeed, some of its advice to men is premised on the possibility of women being the better judges of character, and adept at following suitable behaviour more intuitively than men.

The *Kama Sutra* indicates that there was far more on the Indian male's agenda than mere sexual conquest: they were required to cultivate themselves in poetry, music, clothing and even personal hygiene. The text reveals a world of urban sophistication in which men and women are in constant interaction, manoeuvring for advantage, passionately engaging with each other through every fibre of their bodies and minds. Vatsyayana – or the many writers who are identified through this single name – wholeheartedly endorses a life that is filled with pleasure and aesthetic delight. Yet he is no dissolute seeker of sensation. His ideal relationship is marriage, albeit one in which physical pleasure is a wholesome presence. He is uncertain about the point at which relationships become sinful; careful about when condemnation is necessary, he cleverly steers his male reader through the reality of social temptations while subtly suggesting when they would transgress moral codes. With the endorsement of marriage, he intelligently locates pleasures and acute sensibility within a more stately code of social responsibility and appropriate conduct – in a word, within *dharma* (ethical conduct). It was left to those who followed to interpret the relative importance of pleasure and ethics within their own lives.

Ancient Indian life is presented through the *Kama Sutra* as being joyously worldly, but contained within a complex ethical framework set in turn against a sweeping, austere and grand spiritual vision.

YOGA: A DIVINE DISCIPLINE

The Sanskrit word *yoga* (literally, "yoke"), originally referred simply to practice, but practice as it related specifically to a spiritual life. In the *Mahabharata*, the concept was described as having four aspects, which formed the basis of all subsequent theories and uses of the discipline: preparation through ethical conduct and personal purity; precisely held physical postures; meditative techniques; and withdrawal from the sensory and psychological grasp of the world. In the *Bhagavad Gita*, the term yoga is used to refer to various disciplines in spiritual life, and the text talks of the yogas of action, inquiry and devotion.

The theory of yoga that has been handed down to modern times was first systematized in the collection of short statements known as the *Yoga Sutra* (first century BCE), attributed to Patanjali; the theory outlined in the text was gradually developed in subsequent commentaries over the next one thousand years. In this work, yoga is presented as a precise collection of highly disciplined practices for controlling the entire human being in such a way as to bring freedom from the restraints of the world. The yogic practices are designed to treat the individual holistically as an integral being, addressing together those aspects that modern Western thought understands separately as physical, mental, psychological and spiritual. In yoga, long practice in gaining and holding demanding poses is not just a matter of becoming supple and healthy; the physical changes have a direct impact on how much control a person has over his or her thoughts and inclinations. Likewise, meditative techniques – such as concentrating your mind on an imaginary flame behind closed eyes – are not only mental contests to subdue the vagaries of thought, but are also concerned with heightening the wellbeing of the body. Divisions are not made in yoga, as all these different levels work toward a balanced individual.

But what was the practice of yoga principally intended for? The answer in the classical texts is as unclear as it is now. It is posited that yoga enabled individuals to free themselves from the restraints of the material world – but what does this really imply? The strict spiritual explanation is that freedom meant that the individual self never needed to be born again into another life and would be released from the endless cycle of death and rebirth (*samsara*). Yoga was therefore the deliberate withdrawal from the world into a state of purified consciousness which, upon death, would ensure liberation from *karma* (the consequences of past deeds) and rebirth. But a wider folk belief was that such freedom meant becoming a master of the forces of the world rather than their slave. Popular narratives attributed great powers to sages who had practiced yoga: it was believed that they could command natural phenomena and animals to do their bidding, they could read minds, see the future, talk to the gods, and so on.

There was also, however, a more pragmatic understanding of yoga, which coincides with the modern perception of it: freedom from the restraints of the world meant not being subjected to its shocks and pressures – tension, sadness, anxiety, uncertainty and the like. The practitioner of yoga would be empowered to gain a distance from the events and circumstances that cause suffering and be able to enjoy a full and balanced life. Yoga would not lead to distance from the world, nor to mastery over it, but rather to a calm and clear engagement with it. Thus understood, different styles of yoga spread through Hindu, Buddhist and Jain practices.

LEFT **Although lord of the dance, Shiva is a tranquil ascetic, in whose meditative consciousness the universe lies waiting to be born – and in this capacity, he is identified as the lord of yoga. In this 18th-century painting from Murshidabad he is depicted in eight different yogic postures. Iconographically, note the cobra around his body and the Ganges flowing from his head. (The figure at the top left here appears to be the androgynous form of Shiva, Ardhanarishvara.)**

AN ORAL TRADITION

BELOW A 15th-century
manuscript of the sacred
Rig Veda ("Wisdom of the
Verses"), the oldest of the
four *Veda*s (compiled ca.
1500–1100BCE). The text was,
and still is, transmitted
orally, but even before the
advent of modern printing,
it was occasionally
rendered into writing,
using the *devanagari* script
in which Sanskrit is
recorded.

Although soapstone seals found by the thousand among the ruins of the Indus civilization of the third millennium BCE reveal that the ancient culture had its own written language, their pictographic symbols remain undeciphered. Sanskrit, a Proto-Indo-European language, is the earliest understood Indian tongue. Sanskrit's earliest literature appears to date from about 1800BCE and it has remained the sacred language of Hindus ever since.

The *Veda*s (ca. 1500–1100BCE) are made up of the *Rig Veda*, a collection of hymns; the *Yajur Veda*, a body of sacrificial formulas; the *Sama Veda*, a set of ritual chants; and the *Atharva Veda*, which contains spells and incantations. Each *Veda* is divided into four sections: *Samhita*s, *Brahmana*s, *Aranyaka*s, and *Upanishad*s. The *Samhita*s are hymns or *mantra*s (sacred words). *Brahmana*s are collections of prose

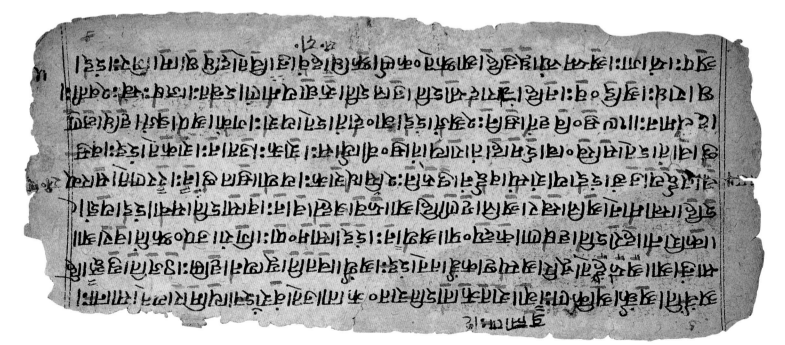

writings that describe sacrificial rites. The *Aranyaka*s and *Upanishad*s (ca. 1200–600BCE) focused more on interpreting the meaning of religious experience.

The language of all these works was Sanskrit, which had crystallized enough into such a systematic and internally coherent language that by the fifth to the fourth centuries BCE, it had received its authoritative grammar, the *Astadhayayi* by Panini. The script in which it came to be written developed out of and superseded Brahmi (the first Indian script) and was called *devanagari* ("ornament of the gods"). The plays of Kalidasa, Sudraka, Bhana and others from the Gupta period and after (the fourth to the seventh centuries CE) were usually written down. Nonetheless, the purely oral tradition of Hinduism continued to preserve its ancient nature, not only in Sanskrit but also in other languages. The challenge to Sanskrit had come in the time of the Buddha and Mahavira, who spoke in Prakrit, Sauraseni and Magadhi. The Buddha's teachings were recorded in another popular fourth-century language, Pali. But Sanskrit had, by the very nature of its priestly, philosophical and esoteric elitism, not been a common language. The latter changed over the centuries and by 1000CE new successor languages had evolved, including Hindi, Bengali, Kashmiri and Gujarati.

Sanskrit had slowly penetrated South India, but there was already a dominant classical language there, Tamil. In the first millennium of the Common Era, Tamil rapidly established a wide corpus of secular poetry, drama and theoretical works, as well as religious manuals and poetry; and although it remained primarily an oral literature, it was constantly written and re-written in perishable palm leaves in its own ancient script. It interacted creatively with Sanskrit, out of which emerged the southern languages of Malayalam, Kannada and Telugu with (by the eleventh to the twelfth centuries) their own literature and scripts.

THE GREAT STORIES

BELOW The sage Vyasa (centre right), legendary author of the *Mahabharata,* is shown dictating the contents of the epic poem to the elephant-headed deity Ganesha (centre left). The goddess Durga, astride a tiger, and the four-headed Brahma are also represented in this 18th-century painting.

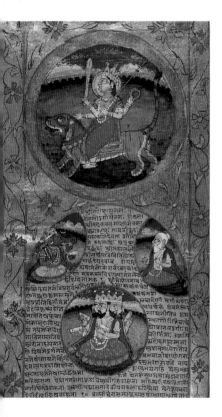

The earliest Hindu texts were "heard" (*sruti*), and contrasted with those that recorded events or thoughts remembered by their authors and were therefore classified as "recollection" (*smrti*). This large category took in works that were classified in different ways. Although conventionally referred to as the two "epics", the *Ramayana* was classified as a "poem" (*kavya*) and the *Mahabharata* as "history" (*itihasa* – "thus-happened"). The *Ramayana* (third century BCE to fourth century CE) emerged as a coherent narrative song of wandering minstrels. The *Mahabharata,* on the other hand, is a compendium of stories that was popular and widely circulated over the centuries of its formation (third century BCE to fifth century CE). Another vast body of texts classified as *smrti* were the narratives of the gods, most important of which were the theologically self-conscious accounts of the nature and actions of Vishnu, Shiva and the Devi known as the *Purana*s ("antiquities" or "of the past"). They were compiled, between the fourth and the twelfth centuries CE, from narrative myths and regional stories from all over India.

Originally entitled *Jaya* ("Victory"), the *Mahabharata* ("The Great Story of Bharata") is an examination of *dharma* (ethical conduct) that centres on an account of the bloody struggle between rival dynasties of cousins, the immoral Kauravas and the dutiful Pandavas, for a single throne. With some 100,000 couplets, it is the world's longest epic poem – around seven times longer than the western epics the *Iliad* and the *Odyssey* put together. This great work was ascribed to Vyasa (whose name means "Compiler"), a priest who retired to a Himalayan cave where he dictated the poem to the elephant-headed god Ganesha over a period of two-and-a-half years. The historical understanding is that the poem was compiled by many different writers from a vast range of materials including mythology, philosophy and

RIGHT In this spirited 16th-century painting illustrating a battle scene in the *Bhagavad Gita,* the gods look down on the mortal hero Arjuna (far right), who is directed and assisted by his personal charioteer (and God incarnate), Krishna (second from right), during the climactic engagement with the Kauravas at Kurukshetra. Krishna fortifies the will of the wavering Arjuna, convincing him at his moment of moral crisis that it is his duty to proceed and to fight for what is right.

hero stories. A wealth of mythical and instructive material remains in the epic because, despite its salience, the narrative of the cousins' struggle takes up only one-fifth of the poem. So diverse and far-reaching is the text, so enmeshed in its native culture, that there is a popular saying that no Indian ever hears the *Mahabharata* for the first time.

The climax of the Kaurava–Pandava story is a great battle at Kurukshetra between the rival cousins. Prior to the battle, the heroic Pandava warrior, Arjuna, is unsure whether he should proceed and is advised on his *dharma* (ethical duty) as a warrior by Krishna, his enigmatic charioteer cousin. Krishna offers profound insights on the right way to live, and then reveals himself to Arjuna as God. This episode is contained in a separate eighteen-chapter episode, the *Bhagavad Gita* ("The Song of the Blessed"). Krishna argues that there are three different but complementary ways to achieve release from the cycle of birth and death: first, by acting according to one's *dharma* but with detachment from selfish desire; second, by pursuing knowledge and withdrawing from the world; and third, through worship on the path of devotion.

Dharma, in the sense of the dictates of honour and the precedence of convention and tradition over personal interests, also plays a major role in the other great Sanskrit epic, the *Ramayana*. It tells the tale of Rama, a

RIGHT **Rama, the hero of the *Ramayana* and the *avatar* (incarnation) of the god Vishnu, is represented in this 18th-century painting with all the attributes of idealized masculinity. He is shown sitting on the shoulders of the faithful monkey Hanuman, while fighting off the demonic Ravana, the kidnapper of Rama's beloved wife, Sita.**

prince of Ayodhya, who wins the hand of Princess Sita, the epitome of purity. On the eve of his accession, the couple is denied the throne and cast into exile by Rama's father. As they roam the wilderness, Sita is kidnapped by the demon-king Ravana and taken to the kingdom of Lanka. Rama spends years searching for her before he eventually rescues her with the help of his monkey ally Hanuman and obliterates the demon. Yet the time spent by Sita in the company of another man has brought Rama dishonour, and he asks her to demonstrate her purity. She enters a fire that leaves her unblemished; and they return to Ayodhya to rule. Although the *Ramayana* is a tale of martial glory, centred on an ideal warrior who clearly draws the lines between good and evil, it is also a corpus of moral and ethical precepts that provides a guide to statesmanship, human conduct and relationships.

This trend towards devotionalism had its culmination in the development of accessibly written books of instructions, theological concepts, legends, myths, cosmology, and genealogies known as the *Puranas*. This was an era of competition between rival Hindu sects and the texts are generally grouped by scholars according to whether they celebrate Vishnu or Shiva, and later, Devi, the Great Goddess. Of particular interest is a South Indian example, the *Bhagavata Purana*, which probably dates from the ninth or tenth century CE. This influential work embraces an intense devotionalism, notably in its description of the god Krishna's childhood among the forest cowherds of Vrindavan, his youthful pranks, and his dalliance with the wives and daughters of the cowherds (the *gopis*). By this time, Krishna was established as an incarnation of Vishnu and the poem makes much of his mischievousness, beauty and unpredictability. The lyrical description of the *gopis*' pining for the beautiful young man is a moving image of the human soul's longing for union with God.

EMPIRES OF SPIRIT AND SWORD

LEFT With all the pomp and circumstance associated with such occasions, Sadullah Khan, prime minister during the reign of Shah Jahan (1628–1657), is shown in this illustration, ca. 1655, presiding over a formal ceremonial gathering, possibly involving either foreign visitors or internal ministers with whom he is discussing affairs of state. Shah Jahan's rule was characterized by religious tolerance and relative political stability. He is, however, probably best remembered for the construction of the Taj Mahal, widely regarded as one of the most exquisite of all Muslim tombs (see pages 90–91).

Temporal and spiritual power, this world and the next, kings and priests, edicts and scriptures, great and small cultures – all weave together to reveal the complex and colourful interactions of India's past. No single faith or empire can adequately express all that was India; so we must look beyond this, at the many empires – of the spirit and of the sword – that have been born in, or entered and made this ancient land. To understand India, it is necessary to make sense of the profusion of beliefs and practices that is "Hinduism". But Jainism, Buddhism and Sikhism also arose in the country, and both Islam and Christianity have long and complex histories there. Aside from its many religions, India's kingdoms and empires are so numerous that those which follow are only some of the most influential formations over the millennia.

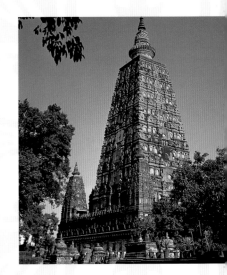

BELOW The Mahabodhi temple at Bodhgaya was completed in the 14th century near the site of the Bodhi tree under which the Buddha is believed to have attained enlightenment.

JAINISM

J ainism is derived from the Sanskrit *jina*, meaning "conqueror" – a reference to the triumphant self-perfection of its great teacher, Mahavira, against the impurities, restrictions, temptations and suffering of the world. Jains believe that by austere means it is possible for individuals to overcome mind, passion and body and attain deliverance from the endless cycle of rebirth. Jainism's five vows are not to lie, not to steal, to be chaste, not to have possessions and to practice non-violence. This rigorous code of existence is believed to enable a person to become free of the cycle of lives. Jains sought philosophically to establish their position through a careful understanding of others, and socially to interact peacefully with other communities while at the same time preserving their own rituals and identity.

The Jain tradition owes its major features to the teachings of Mahavira (ca. 599–527BCE), the last of its twenty-four *tirthankaras* or "fordbuilders" – those who attained perfect wisdom by breaking all bonds with this world. Except for the last two *tirthankaras*, Parshva (877–777BCE) and Mahavira, all these figures inhabited the world millennia ago. Mahavira was probably an older contemporary of the Buddha. Both came from the princely warrior class (*kshatriya*) and sought truth through ascetic meditation. But whereas Mahavira stressed the need for rigorous asceticism, the Buddha taught the "Middle Way": a balance between over-eager engagement with the world and what he said was too obsessive a path of self-denial.

There are two main sects in Jainism, a division which arose out of the issue of whether clothing was excessive for an ascetic: the Shvetambara (the larger) wear white, while the Digambara go naked. There are many Jaina sacred texts, but the most significant one is considered to be the *Tattvartha Sutra* ("That Which Is"), recorded in the second century CE by the monk-scholar Umaswami.

Jainism was particularly influential in South India between the third and the seventh centuries and in eastern North India between the ninth and the twelfth centuries. Almost invariably written in accessible languages rather than in Sanskrit, it flourished in regional cultures. But the efflorescence of Tamil Hindu devotionalism between the seventh and the tenth centuries marginalized Jainism in the South; and the defeat of the major Jain kings of Bengal in the eleventh century was also a catastrophe. Thereafter, Jainism remained a vibrant religion only in the western region of Gujarat and in some pockets of Karnataka in South India.

BUDDHISM

Siddhartha Gautama (ca. 566–486BCE) was a northern Indian *kshatriya* (warrior), son of the chief of the Shakya tribe. In the standard Buddhist narrative, Siddhartha's father tried to shield him from unhappiness and confined him to the palace grounds. But when Siddhartha succeeded in leaving the palace for the first time he was shocked by "Four Sights" that opened his eyes to the suffering of the world: an old man, a sick man, a corpse and a begging monk. Siddhartha abandoned

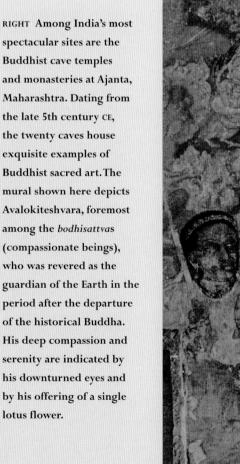

RIGHT **Among India's most spectacular sites are the Buddhist cave temples and monasteries at Ajanta, Maharashtra. Dating from the late 5th century CE, the twenty caves house exquisite examples of Buddhist sacred art. The mural shown here depicts Avalokiteshvara, foremost among the *bodhisattvas* (compassionate beings), who was revered as the guardian of the Earth in the period after the departure of the historical Buddha. His deep compassion and serenity are indicated by his downturned eyes and by his offering of a single lotus flower.**

his old existence to seek the meaning of what he had seen, adopting the life of a wandering ascetic or *sramana*. After six years, he sat in meditation until he "awakened" to the truth. His teaching (the first sermon delivered in Sarnath, called the "Setting of the Wheel of Dharma in Motion") became known as the "Four Noble Truths": life is suffering; desire (or more tellingly, thirst) is the cause of suffering; the cessation of desire is the cessation of suffering; and the cessation of suffering is achieved through the "Eightfold Path" (right views, right intention, right speech, right action, right way of life, right effort, right awareness and right concentration). Once this path was followed, desire would cease, and so would suffering. But since suffering is the very nature of life, its cessation would mean the vanishing of life and the cycle of lives. This is *nirvana* – an "extinction" or "putting out" of that cycle. Like Jainism, Buddhist ethics formulated five precepts – no killing, no stealing, no lying, no abusive sex and no intoxicating beverages – but these were expanded over time.

Although influenced by Vedic cosmology, Buddhism developed its own system, according to which the Earth was centred on Mount Meru (see page 40); beneath its peak stretched an underground realm of 136 hells, each set aside for the punishment of a particular wrongdoing. From the summit could be seen the lands of the four great kings, Kubera, Virudhaka, Dhritarashtra and Virupaksha, rulers of north, south, east and west respectively. Above was the heaven of Shakra, counterpart to the *Rig Veda*'s thunder god Indra, and forty-four other heavens. Higher still than these celestial realms was the abode of those who had achieved enlightenment and reached the state known as *nirvana*. But this elaborate cosmology grew more in response to popular cultural expectation of mythic narrative than because it had any integral connection to the teaching of the Buddha.

RIGHT A gilt-bronze statue of an affluent-looking Maitreya, the future incarnation of the Buddha. The figure is identifiable by the *stupa* in his crown. It is noteworthy that his rich attire contrasts starkly with the simple dress traditionally used in depictions of the Buddha. Dating from the Pallava dynasty period (7th–9th centuries), the figure was produced near what is today the city of Madras.

The Buddha had criticized caste distinctions and the role of the priestly elite; he encouraged his disciples not to idolize him but to find solutions to their problems based on their own experiences. Despite these entreaties, the Buddha himself was placed increasingly at the heart of the faith as it developed. But the older Theravada ("Doctrine of the Elders") tradition adhered in the main to the early, austere understanding of the Buddha as someone who had gained insight into life and taught it to the world before attaining *moksha* (final release) from *samsara* (the cycle of rebirth) himself. So, while the Buddha is most certainly to be respected, there is no sense in which he is to be prayed to, for he has gone beyond this world.

By the beginning of the first century CE, an alternative strand of Buddhism arose known as the Mahayana ("Greater Vehicle"). It expanded the notion of buddhahood beyond the Buddha by means of a significant mythology relating to *bodhisattva*s, compassionate individuals who had achieved enlightenment but who chose to postpone their entry into *nirvana* in order to help others toward release from rebirth. Two of the most significant *bodhisattva*s were Avalokiteshvara ("the Lord who looks in all directions") and Maitreya, the future incarnation of the Buddha who would usher in the end of the universe's current phase of existence when the teachings of the Buddha had fallen away entirely.

Despite the popularity of these figures in North India over several centuries, Buddhism came under intense pressure from an emerging Hindu religion that combined royal patronage, brahmanical theological exposition and popular devotional practices. Severely attenuated by the eleventh century, Buddhism might have continued to exist in a low-keyed and somewhat marginal accommodation with Hindu culture, but it collapsed finally under the sudden onslaught of Islam in that time.

RIGHT A 1st-century BCE limestone panel depicting the Buddha's footprints, from the Great Stupa at Amaravati, Andhra Pradesh. After the Buddha's death, those who followed in his footsteps continued the practice of forest retreats, which developed into permanent monastic settlements, or *viharas*. Contributions from those in secular society enabled these communities to become increasingly wealthy. With royal patronage, Buddhism was enmeshed in Indian society and played a formative role in helping to define Hindu culture. Feet themselves have long been the focus of rituals of respect in India.

THE THREE BASKETS

A vast literature has been generated by Buddhism, although much of it is very difficult to place historically. But the so-called Pali canon of scripture, known as the *Tipitaka*, and in Sanskrit as the *Tripitaka*, is impressive. Translating as the "Three Baskets", the canon is composed of the *Vinaya Pitaka*, the *Sutta Pitaka* and the *Abhidhamma Pitaka*, a collection of *agamas*, or *nikaya suttas*, or *sutras* (discourses attributed to the Buddha and his early followers). The *Vinaya Pitaka* records the rules of monastic conduct; the *Sutta Pitaka* consists of discourses of the Buddha, including his five collections or Nikayas; and the *Abhidhamma Pitaka* presents his further teachings. The orally inherited teachings were written down in the first century CE, and the Theravada ("Doctrine of Elders") tradition, centred on Sri Lanka (where the Pali canon was taken by Ashoka's son, Mahinda), bases its doctrine entirely on this repository of material, which is

LEFT A 2nd-century CE limestone roundel depicting the *Mandhata Jataka*, from the Great Stupa at Amaravati, Andhra Pradesh. Contained within the *Sutta Pitaka* – one of the three texts that constitute the Pali canon or "Three Baskets" – was a version of the *Jataka* tales. These stories have become so deeply ingrained in Indian culture that in recent years they have been popularized in comic-book form. The story depicted in this roundel is of Mandhata, a wealthy *chacravartin* (universal king). Despite his riches and power, he was constantly dissatisfied and always subject to desire and craving. Shown here is the moment at which Shakra, king of the gods, offers to share his throne with him. Yet even this heavenly role did not satisfy Mandhata and he returned to Earth to die. The tale encapsulates the Buddhist belief that all desire leads to suffering.

believed by scholars to be the most historically authentic in existence. Other schools, such as the Mahayana ("Greater Vehicle"), incorporate these works but have enlarged their corpus during Buddhism's expansion beyond India, principally through their Sanskrit *sutra*s, several of which gave rise to specific East Asian sects. In addition to the supposed utterances of the Buddha himself there are many commentaries and treatises in both Pali and Sanskrit.

Among the oldest of Buddhist scriptures is the *Sutta Pitaka* ("Basket of Discourse"), which is recorded in the ancient Indian language of Pali and contains five collections of discourses said to have been given by the Buddha himself – each is presented as the report of one of the Buddha's disciples and begins with the statement, "This I have heard". Part of the *Sutta Pitaka* is the Dhammapada (in Pali, "The Truthful Way"), an anthology of ethical teachings as delivered in aphoristic style by the Buddha. In Pali, the book has 423 stanzas in twenty-three chapters; there are also extant and slightly different versions in Sanskrit, Prakrit and Chinese. The *Sutta Pitaka* also contains an example of the *Jataka* tales, which developed into a popular genre, retelling accounts of the previous lives of the Buddha.

Buddhism had a major role to play in the development of Indian philosophy (see pages 128–129): as the Buddhist thinkers of the Mahayana tradition began to engage with the early phases of systematic Hindu (or more properly, brahminical) philosophy, they changed to writing in Sanskrit. Over the first millennium, Buddhist philosophy was an integral part of the intellectual scene, sometimes being treated with surprising sympathy by brahminical opponents, but certainly indirectly complimented by having its advances in logic, theory of knowledge and philosophy of language adopted and adapted by Hindu schools.

ISLAM

The faith of Islam (Arabic for "submission") originated through a series of revelations from God received by a merchant, Muhammad ibn Abdallah, who lived in Mecca amid the deserts of the Arabian peninsula in the seventh century. These revelations, collected together as the Quran, are held to be God's direct word to the true Prophet, Muhammad; their dissemination inspired the conversion of then pagan tribal Arabia. Islam was subsequently spread beyond the immediate region by its followers, known as Muslims (from a word meaning "to submit"), who believed they were submitting to and enacting the divine will of bringing order to the universe. Muslim rulers absorbed Persia, Afghanistan and Central Asia and reached northern India between the eighth and the eleventh centuries.

Islam had first come to the southwestern coast of peninsular India through Arab traders, and then by armies invading what is now Sind in Pakistan. India's first major experience of Islam was in the eleventh century when the Ghaznavids established a vast empire in what is today western Iran and Afghanistan, under their formidable leader Mahmud. Although Mahmud and succeeding armies were skilful, they were assisted by the absence of any powerful empire in North India. Actual Muslim rule on any extensive scale reached India in the late twelfth century with the establishment of Muslim authority in the three-hundred-year-old settlement of Delhi, which they destroyed and rebuilt. This came to be called the Delhi Sultanate.

Islam's monotheism and opposition to image worship made it the antithesis of mainstream Hinduism in which unity was multiplicity and diversity was celebrated; unlike Jainism, Islam's essential message was that it presented the one and only truth (although in practice it was never monolithic). Furthermore, the interpretation of war as a holy duty to spread the teachings of Islam lent psychologically

RIGHT This 16th-century Indo-Persian style painting on cotton cloth is one of approximately 1,400 pieces originally commissioned by the Mughal emperor Akbar to illustrate the *Adventures of Hamza*, or *Hamzanama*. The hero is based on the character of Amir Hamza, an uncle of the Prophet Muhammad, who became the focus of popular legends related in performance by storytellers. In these tales the intrepid Hamza experienced many adventures as he travelled the world to spread the word of Islam. Only about 140 illustrations survive – this one depicts a series of miraculous incidents that were said to have taken place at the birth of Muhammad ibn Abdallah, the Prophet Muhammad.

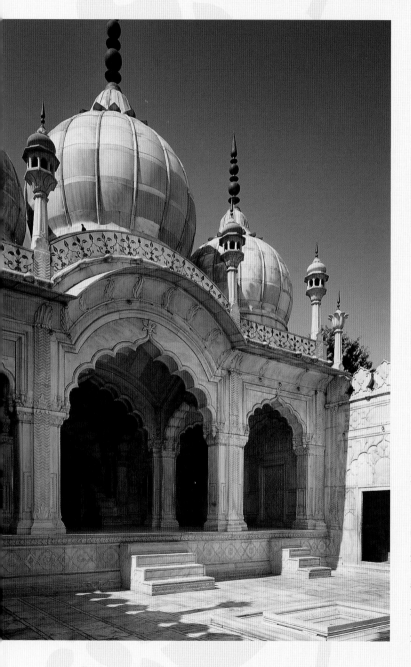

potent weight to the political and economic motivation of the invaders. Hindu kings had destroyed temples in enemy kingdoms before, but the Muslim armies took this practice to a new scale, with new purpose. The destruction and looting of temples extended to a theological demonstration: the images were desecrated in a way few Hindu rulers would have conceived of doing. But despite occasional outbursts of violent conversion, the spread of Islam in India was piecemeal and peaceful. Once a Muslim power had conquered territory it permitted other faiths to remain, but subjected them to onerous taxes. A social division gradually formed between the *ashraf* (the Muslims of foreign origin) and the *ajlaf* (the Indian converts), with the former preserving a sense of superiority.

Several factors contributed to Islam's increasing popularity in India from the eleventh century onward: escape from the restrictions of the Hindu class structure, the appeal of opportunities reserved for Muslims, and the freshness of newly available theological certainties. In the western reaches and northern heartlands of India, and later in the east in Bengal, long under Muslim rule, well

LEFT **The Red Fort at Agra, commissioned during the reign of Shah Jahan and built between 1640 and 1648, served not only as a palace but also as the administrative centre and spiritual artery of the Mughal Empire for more than 200 years. It takes its name from the colossal red sandstone walls, some as high as 110 feet (34m), that surround the palace complex. Within these massive walls is a series of separate pavilions, each with a specific function. One of the most grand and spectacular of all the buildings is the Moti Masjid, shown here. Made of white marble, the ancient mosque takes on different tones according to the time of day – in former years it was said to shine like a magnificent pearl.**

over a third of the population was Muslim; in the central regions of the Deccan, which formed Muslim kingdoms independent of Delhi, perhaps under a quarter; in the South, which hardly ever saw systematic Muslim rule, a very small minority.

But from relatively early in its history in India, Islam began to adapt to its new contexts. While there was an upsurge of popular expressions of self-conscious Hindu literature and practice, under the rubric of the Bhakti (devotional) movement, these also assimilated Islamic ideas.

One aspect of Islam that converts were attracted to was its mystical strand known as Sufism, which had much in common with existing Hindu notions of emotional love of the divine, the possibility of intense mystical trances, the interpretation of sacred teachings through personal experience and a God immanent in the human world. Sufi sects had started throughout the Muslim world, led by ascetics who engaged in an inner quest for spiritual awareness and greater proximity to the divine, for which they often became celebrated in the manner of saints. India became the birthplace of several of the seventeen established Sufi sects, and over the centuries many differences grew up between them. Some of the Indian Sufi groups, such as the Chisti and Qadiri, interacted significantly with Hindu ideas, and drew the suspicion and hostility of the authoritative if loosely defined body of men known as the *ulama* ("learned ones"), interpreters of Islam, because they seemed to deviate from orthodoxy. Other groups were considered not to stand apart from the mainstream, but to offer an example of what it meant in practice to effect a sincere relationship with the divine, as the Prophet Muhammad himself had. The most creative and peaceful interaction between Islam and Hinduism came through common respect for the Sufi saints, who seemed to amalgamate the two traditions.

FLORAL ART

While Islamic art in Arabia adhered strictly to geometric decoration, in obeyance of an interpretation of scripture thought to prohibit organic representation, Islamic art in Persia and India used a variety of naturalistic floral and vegetal motifs. Examples range from the forms used by Mansur and Abu'l Hasan in the inlay décor of the women's section of Shah Jahan's palace fort at Delhi and in the Taj Mahal (see illustration, page 32), to the delicate gold, silver and black metalwork on bowls (as in the example above). Many everyday objects of exquisite beauty were created during the Mughal era, such as these ornamented turban pins (left and right) and this white nephrite jade pot (opposite) embellished with inset ruby-and-gold floral motifs.

THE MAURYAS AND BEYOND

The first great empire of Indian history was created by the Maurya dynasty when Chandragupta Maurya established himself in Pataliputra in 320BCE. By 305BCE he had extended his territory over most of Afghanistan, Baluchistan and the Indus Valley. He appears to have abdicated, giving way to his son Bindushara, and joined a company of Jain monks, with whom he travelled to southern India, where he is said to have starved himself to death according to the highest ideal of Jain spiritual austerity. However, his ascent and ingenious establishment of a vast empire is traditionally tied to the support and ideas of his minister, Kautilya, author of the brilliant manual on kingship, political administration, foreign policy and diplomacy called the *Artha Shastra* ("Science of Objectives"). Pataliputra appears to have been the largest city on Earth at the time of Chandragupta Maurya's rule, twice as large as Rome at the height of its empire five hundred years later.

In 261BCE, his grandson Ashoka set off to consolidate the eastern frontier regions. But he felt remorse at the devastation and bloodshed he had caused: "a hundred thousand people deported … many times that number perished". Thereafter he embraced the Buddhist faith, renounced war and sought to convert the peoples of his empire to a similar code of ethics (see page 20).

After Ashoka, the empire collapsed. Kushana merchants established trading relations with the Roman Empire and their usually Buddhist (but occasionally also Shiva-worshipping) kings fostered the great university of Takshila in what is now Afghanistan. Although there was no large and stable political formation in India, the period between the second century BCE and the third century CE was one of great cultural, philosophical, literary and commercial activity. Key works across every genre were composed at this time – from portions of the *Ramayana* and the

Mahabharata (see pages 56–59) to the authoritative Law Code of Manu (the *Manu Smrti*) to the seminal texts of the philosophical schools, including of the newly developed Mahayana ("Greater Vehicle") Buddhism. Northern India was the fulcrum of trans-Asian trade. In the deep South, small but apparently peaceful kingdoms built up a massive trade surplus against the Roman Empire through trade in spices and other precious commodities. In the Tamil country, significant gold hoards have been discovered, many of them struck for a first-century CE king of the Pandya kingdom, who was styled Roma-puri Pandyan (the "Pandya of the City of Rome").

LEFT The capital of Ashoka's most famous column – the one erected at Sarnath, site of the Buddha's first sermon (see page 65). Its symbols stand atop an inverted lotus and consist of a 24-spoked Dharma wheel alongside an elephant, a bull, a horse, and a lion – animals thought to represent stages of the Buddha's life (conception, desire, departure and attainment of buddhahood). Four lions, symbolizing kingship, face the cardinal directions.

THE GUPTA GOLDEN AGE

RIGHT **A 4th–5th-century terracotta roundel, from Uttar Pradesh. By the Gupta period, Hindu temples were either small stone buildings or more elaborate structures made of brick and decorated with terracotta panels. During this era, the Hindu practice of worshipping images of the gods became established, as did the standard layout of the Hindu temple, with a courtyard and a central shrine, the *garbhagriha* ("womb house"), in which the image of the deity was kept in shadowy halflight. The temple tower was pioneered by Gupta architects. Many fine Buddhas were also carved, and the magnificent rock-cut temple caves and monasteries at Ajanta in western India, with their exquisite fresco paintings (see page 64), flourished under Gupta rule.**

The Guptas established a new empire in northern India, ushering in a "golden age" in which philosophy, literature, sculpture, architecture and other arts and sciences flowered. Chandra Gupta I (r. 320–335CE), Samudra Gupta (r. 335–370CE) and Chandra Gupta II (r. 375–415CE) built an empire that ran from the Deccan to the Himalayas and from Dhaka to Karachi. The triumphs of Samudra Gupta are elaborately described in the *Allahabad Inscription* and in the fourth canto of the poem the *Raghuvamsa* by the peerless Kalidasa, who represents the conquests as those of

the legendary Raghu, ancestor of Rama (hero of the *Ramayana* and *avatar* of Vishnu).

The idea that kings were gods (which had come from Greece and Persia into the ruling ideology of the Kushanas and others) was drawn upon by the Guptas. Their innovation lay in melding this with the narratives of Hindu deities and the idealized requirements of the Dharma texts. They became the first – and in terms of geographical spread, the only – truly Hindu emperors and strove self-consciously to realize in their administrative structures, military conduct, public ritual and royal persona the ideal of themselves as inheritors of the divine rulers of the mythic past. They created a coherent high Hindu culture across their empire, but they were nevertheless also supportive of Buddhism and Jainism.

The Vaishnavas (followers of the Hindu god Vishnu) received full recognition from the Gupta kings, who adopted the title Paramabhagavata ("divinely blessed [by God]"). At the same time, the ancient cult of the Mother Goddess, linked to local fertility deities, became increasingly popular – Durga, consort of Shiva, was an important religious force from the fourth century CE onward.

The administrative structures of the Guptas remained the dominant model for Hindu rulers. Their power began to decline as the Roman Empire and the trade routes collapsed under the onslaught of the nomadic Huns, who were repeatedly repelled by the great Gupta emperors. But wars of succession in the middle of the sixth century weakened the Gupta Empire significantly, and the Huns finally succeeded in breaking through. The geography of Indian power, centred on Pataliputra since before the Mauryas, never recovered from the devastation. Ancient India and the Classical Age that was its heir disappeared, leaving behind only their religious and philosophical influence for the ages to come.

REGIONAL POWERS

The first considerable kingdom after the Guptas was built by Harsha (r.606–647CE) at Kanauj, north of Delhi. Although his empire collapsed on his death, Kanauj remained the imperial centre of North India for several centuries, being the capital of the Gurjara Pratihara kingdom, which survived until the onslaught from Muslim invaders in the eleventh century. In this period, eastern India began to gain its own place in the country's history, with a succession of independent kingdoms similar to the Palas (in the eighth to the twelfth centuries).

In South India, an ancient Tamil culture existed with a traditional division between three peoples, the Chola, the Chera and the Pandya. In the central uplands stretching into the Deccan plateau, several dynasties emerged after the decline of the Guptas, notably the Satavahana. But the most significant kingdom was that of the Chalukya of Badami, who strove to control much of central India and part of the South between the seventh and eighth centuries.

A previously unknown dynasty, the Pallava, suddenly grew to prominence in the Tamil land in the seventh to the eighth centuries. It was under the Pallavas that Tamil literature grew from ancient, localized texts into a complex hybrid of Sanskrit religion and Tamil sensibilities. This literature came to be associated with a new religious outlook, called *bhakti* ("devotion"), in which the emotions of intense human relationships were directed into a person's approach to the divine.

In the ninth century, the Rashtrakutas, a Deccan dynasty, established an empire that stretched briefly into the Indo-Gangetic plains. But the most notable formation of this period was the Chola Empire (ninth to the thirteenth centuries), based in the Tamil city of Tanjavur. Under the legendary Rajaraja I (r.985–1014) and his co-ruler son Rajendra (r.1012–1044), Chola armies reached the Ganges, took over parts of

Sri Lanka and gained control of the trade lines to Southeast Asia. This is the high-watermark of Tamil culture, with the Chola emperors consciously drawing on their ancient Tamil ancestors while at the same time skilfully associating themselves with Sanskritic Hinduism. Buddhism was patronized by Rajaraja, and kept its small place in Tamil culture – its last toehold in India. Hindu theology and Tamil and Sanskrit poetry flourished, as did sophisticated agricultural and trading systems. But the Cholas are best remembered for their temples (see pages 82–83). It was also under them that bronze-casting was perfected, resulting in an expressive and dynamic style of sculpture, which included Shiva as the Lord of the Dance (see page 37).

LEFT **Between the 7th and 8th centuries and the 10th and 12th centuries, much of central and southern India was under the rule of the western and eastern branches of the Chalukyas. The centre of early Chalukyan glory was Badami, the site of several notable rock-cut temples. The picturesque Bhutanatha temple in Badami is shown here, with a view of the temple's platform extending into the east end of the water tank.**

"TEMPLE-CITIES": BRIHADISHVARA

Enormous walled temples – virtually self-contained cities – were built under the southern Indian Chola rulers in the eleventh century. They housed hundreds of shrines, administrative and residential buildings, sites for ritual bathing and even bazaars. The larger temples were important educational centres, employers and artistic patrons. One of the most notable of these temple complexes, with a vast worshipping community, was the Brihadishvara temple (shown here) in the Chola capital Tanjavur.

The temple was built in honour of the god Shiva between 1003 and 1010 CE at the behest of Rajaraja I, the greatest emperor of the dynasty. Two imposing carved gateways led onto a huge courtyard, 500 feet by 250 feet (152m by 76m) in area, surrounded by a thick granite wall bearing 1,008 images of Shiva's attendant, Nandi. The *garbhagriha*, or inner sanctuary, contained a large, simple aniconic Shiva *linga* (phallic emblem) 12 feet (3.6m) tall. Above the sanctuary, a thirteen-story pyramidal tower rose 220 feet (67m), bearing a granite block (*uttamavimana*) and a gold-covered copper *kalasha*, or finial, exactly the same height as the *linga*.

Endowed by Rajaraja with a grant that he had collected in his imperial wars, the temple complex was an immense enterprise, employing hundreds of priests, more than fifty musicians, and 400 *devadasi*s, or dancing women dedicated to the temple, as well as sculptors, poets, singers, painters, cooks, gardeners, carvers, flower-pickers and creators of colourful garlands. The king set aside thousands of acres to keep the temple supplied with food. He made good use of his musicians, introducing the daily singing of Sanskrit and Tamil devotional hymns. Rajaraja named the temple Rajarajesvaramudayar, but it was renamed under the Cholas' successors, the Nayakas.

MUSLIMS AND HINDUS

In 1193 there was a major shift in power and culture in India in the wake of the defeat of Prithviraja Chauhan at the battle of Tarain and the capture and occupation of Delhi by the armies of the Muslim Afghan leader Muhammad of Ghur (see page 18). The dynasty founded after Mahmud's death in 1206 by one of his generals, Qutb ud-Din Aibak (r.1206–1211), initiated a series that together came to be called the Delhi Sultanate (see page 70).

Five other dynasties followed: the Khilji (1290–1320), the Tughluq (1320–1413), the Sayyid (1414–1451), and, finally, the Lodi (1451–1526). The rule of the highly efficient but utterly ruthless Ala ud-Din Khilji (r.1296–1315) marks the Sultanate's high point.

Based in an urban centre remote from the rural and agricultural economies over which it ruled, the Sultanate's administrations neverthe-less oversaw a cultural renaissance that arose from the stimulating interactions between Hin-duism and Islam – an artistic fusion that affected architecture, music, literature and religion.

The Delhi Sultanate could never control

LEFT **To celebrate the triumph of Islam in India, Qutb ud-Din Aibak (r.1206–1211) erected a great tower in Delhi, the Qutb Minar, some 240 feet (73m) in height. It stands on the ruins of Lal Kot, the citadel of the last Hindu rulers of Delhi. Despite the assimilative culture of the subcontinent, this structure served as a significant symbol in the history of the country, marking the end of one era and the birth of a new one.**

India from the Deccan southward, and in 1345 the general Bahman Shah established a sultanate from Gulbarga in Karnataka. The Bahmani Sultanate also demonstrated signs of creativity, especially in architecture, which combined Indian and Persian elements. However, the Sultanate eventually disintegrated into four parts.

The Vijayanagar Empire emerged in the mid-fourteenth century through the efforts of two brothers, Harihara and Bukka. It reached its apogee under Krishnadeva Raya (r.1509–1529) who won every campaign he fought, bringing virtually the whole peninsula under his control. He was an accomplished poet, and his court witnessed the composition of seminal Kannada and Telugu works. Vijayanagar has been described in considerable detail by both Muslim and European sources: it was an extraordinarily prosperous empire, with ordinary people enjoying a far better standard of living than in any other area of India, the Islamic world or Europe at that time. The rulers created a self-consciously Hindu royalty and were active in reviving rituals and offices that went as far back as the ancient texts. Although they saw themselves very clearly as the Hindu resistance to Muslim invasion, Muslims within their borders enjoyed complete freedom. Although mindful of the threat posed by the newly arrived Portuguese on the west coast, they nevertheless hired Europeans for their armies, and allowed European merchants and travellers free movement.

But Vijayanagar eventually collapsed in the wake of the decisive battle of Talikota (1564) against a sudden alliance of the Muslim Deccan states. Beyond its actual downfall, which was brought about by complex circumstances, one apparent feature of the defeat – that Muslim states combined to defeat the last great Hindu kingdom – left the unfortunate impression that the main feature of Indian history was ultimately the struggle between the Hindu and Islamic religions.

THE MUGHAL EMPIRE

Babur, prince of Samarkand, defeated the last of the Delhi Sultans at the battle of Panipat in 1526. Deploying a mobile artillery against a large but ill-organized army, the Mughals were able to enter Delhi and establish the Mughal Empire. Although Babur's son, Humayun, lost his kingdom temporarily to the Afghan chieftain Sher Shah, he regained it soon after the latter's death in 1555.

Humayun's son Akbar ascended the throne in 1556 at the age of thirteen, and went on to become one of the most extraordinary rulers the world has ever seen. He brought Persian, Afghan, Turkish and Indian Muslims together with Punjabi and Rajput Hindus to develop a sophisticated and integrated ruling class that transcended religious differences. In his thirties, Akbar found himself master of land from Bengal in the east to Kandahar in Afghanistan in the west – the farthest west that any Indian empire had ever reached. He then began to consolidate his empire with internal reforms that fused Persian, Afghan and native Indian elements.

Jahangir, Akbar's son, was often cruel and vacillating in his leadership, and some of his signal achievements in diplomacy and administration can actually be credited to his brilliant wife, Nur Jahan. His reign saw the full flowering of the Mughal school of painting, which skilfully incorporated Western techniques into what was already a fusion of Persian and Indian styles (see illustration, page 95).

Shah Jahan (r.1628–1657) inherited his military valour and cultural ambition from his grandfather, Akbar, but he lacked his diplomatic and inter-religious vision. He was a more conservative Muslim, although later in life he was generous toward Hindus. He is best remembered for the Taj Mahal (see pages 90–91), but he commissioned much else besdides, including the Red Fort (see illustration, page 72).

Aurangzeb, Shah Jahan's son, ascended the throne after having imprisoned his

RIGHT This exquisite jade drinking cup, crafted in 1657 for Shah Jahan, is engraved with the title "Sahib Kiran Sani", which means "the Second Lord of the [auspicious] Conjunction [of Venus and Jupiter]". The first lord had been his ancestor Timur, who had originated the title. In the form of a shell or gourd, its handle terminates in the head of an ibex and a large floret-shaped foot.

father and brutally disposed of his brothers. He extended the empire far into the south, bringing more land under one rule than ever before in the history of India. But by his death in 1707, the Mughal Empire was waiting to implode – which it did, viciously assisted by the cataclysmic invasion of Nadir Shah of Persia. India broke into successor states free of the tottering Mughals who were confined to Delhi.

The Hindu resistance to the Mughals had come originally from the Rajputs, clans of martial ruling families spread across northwest India. The Rajput kingdoms did not unite against Muslim invasions, but fought to save their own particular territory. Despite their martial prowess, they could not form an empire of their own.

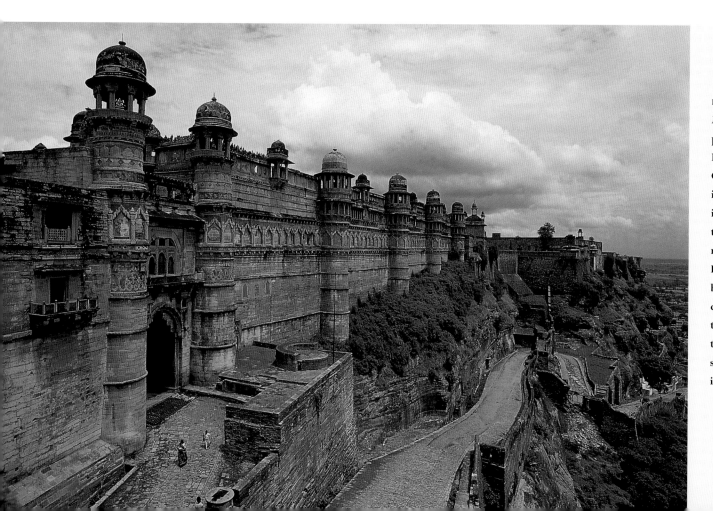

LEFT Described by one Mughal emperor as "... the pearl among fortresses in India", Mahwar Fort at Gwalior, Madhya Pradesh, is undoubtely the most impenetrable structure in the northern and central regions of the country. Built in the 15th century by Man Singh Tomar, it contains six palaces and three temples. A view of the fortress's imposing standstone walls and one of its gates is shown here.

At the collapse of the Sultanate, individual Rajput states attempted to reassert themselves, but were subjugated by Akbar. After Aurangzeb, the old kingdoms – Mewar, Amber, Gwalior and others – rose again, disunited as ever.

In western India, a small community, the Marathas, proved astonishingly able. Under Shivaji, they attacked the European trading post of Surat, drawing the hostile attention of Aurangzeb. Forced to keep his peace with the Mughals, Shivaji consolidated his position, and proclaimed himself king. From then on, he was a thorn in the side of Aurangzeb, presenting himself as the head of a Hindu resistance to the Muslims. He died in 1680. By the time of Aurangzeb's death in 1707, Shivaji's grandson had been made a minor king, but it was his *brahmin* minister (*peshwa*), Baji Rao, who made the Marathas a force in India. Under generations of his family – the Peshwas – the Marathas created a free-wheeling and loose power. They could conquer, but they could not rule. They clearly saw the danger of the European traders who were now using their military to hold small strips of land: but they were eventually eliminated by the British. By the middle of the eighteenth century, India was the scene of a European struggle in which Indian powers played a subsidiary part. An empire did emerge in the country, but it was alien in a way that not even the first Muslim sultans had been, for it ruled from afar. A new age had dawned on this ancient land.

ABOVE **A spectacular room in the Amber Fort near Jaipur, Rajasthan. The walls and ceiling are decorated with marble inlaid with semi-precious stones and exquisite mirrors. Perched high on a ridge, the fort commands extensive views over the surrounding countryside. Built by Raja Man Singh, construction of the fort began in 1592 and was a product of the Rajput resistance to Mughal invasion; it was not completed until the early 18th century, when the threat of Mughal domination was receding.**

THE TAJ MAHAL

When Shah Jahan's wife, Arjuman Banu Begum (known as Mumtaz Mahal), died in childbirth in 1631 the great ruler was devastated and turned his energy to building a tomb worthy of his love for her. Located in Agra, the Taj Mahal took seventeen years to build.

Entirely covered in marble, its four minarets amplify the impact of the dome. The most striking and sublime aspect of the marble facing is the way every passing nuance of light renders the familiar solidity of the building into something new and different each time: a piercingly cool and sharply etched opalescent

under the full moon, a hazy, pale pink at sunrise and a warm rose at sunset. In the burning light of the overhead sun its pristine white blurs into the bleached blue of the sky. The interior and key parts of the surface of the building have exquisite inlay work of semi-precious stones set in vegetal motifs. The light inside the building is diffused magnificently through pierced marble lattices. The subdued air is thick with the memory of an eternal, monumental and colossally solipsistic expression of human love. The poet Rabindranath Tagore described the building as "A teardrop … bright on the cheek of time".

SIKHISM

In the fifteenth century, the meeting of Hindu and Muslim cultures created new forms of religious awareness. Among them was a tradition that combined the Islamic idea of a personal yet formless God with the Hindu practice of intense emotional attachment to the divine. Out of this so-called Sant tradition emerged many notable mystics and savants. Nanak (1469–1539), the founder of Sikhism, was prominent among them for seeking to explain systematically the path to the experience of a mystical union with the divine. He said that God graciously teaches how we may attain the divine through the words of a teacher (*guru*); but additionally, and in a more innovative departure, Nanak conceived this teacher as the *voice* of God in human beings rather than simply as a human being.

A community gradually gathered around Nanak, treating him as their *guru*.

LEFT **The supreme symbol and central place of worship of the Sikh faith is the glorious Golden Temple at Amritsar in the Punjab, northwest India. Guru Arjun devised the architectural plans for the building on land that had been donated to the Sikhs by the Mughal emperor Akbar. The temple was built in 1577, but it was some 200 years after this that the golden dome was added by the Sikh ruler Ranjit Singh.**

A succession of *gurus* followed. By 1606, the time of the fifth *guru*, Arjun, a body of hymns and teachings (known as *Adi Granth* or *Guru Granth Sahib*), from Nanak to Arjun himself, had been compiled and became the primary scripture of the community. It now took itself to be following the *Gurumat* ("the way of life of the Guru"), which is the internal name of Sikhism.

The sixth *guru*, Hargobind, decided to arm the community after the Mughals killed Guru Arjun. In 1699, the tenth *guru*, Gobind Singh, took the organization of the community to an entirely new level. He created the Khalsa, a religious and social order. All men and women who joined it underwent initiation and were obliged to obey a new code of discipline. This included the famous "Five Ks" (*panj kakke*), which referred to *kesh* (uncut hair), *kangha* (comb), *kirpan* (dagger), *kara* (bangle) and *kachha* (short breeches). The wearing of a turban to hold the hair for men was introduced at a somewhat later date. All members of the Khalsa community had one name – men were referred to as Singh ("Lion") and women as Kaur ("Princess") – among their family and personal names.

Before his death in 1708, Guru Gobind Singh announced that the line of *gurus* was ended. Henceforth the *guru* would reside in the *Granth Sahib* and in the Khalsa itself: text and community would be the guide to the individual's spiritual progress.

Another institution that helped to steer the community was the *gurdwara* ("the *guru*'s door"), or the Sikh Temple. Community singing and prayer, as well as feeding, festivity and pastoral care all centred on this building. The most important and famous of all *gurdwara*s is the magnificent Golden Temple in Amritsar, built in 1577 and known as the Harmandir Sahib (after "Hari", the traditional name for Vishnu, which the *gurus* adopted as a name of God).

THE SPIRIT OF THOMAS

India is one of the oldest homes of Christianity, although historians differ as to exactly when it was introduced and how. It is not until the third century CE that there is any mention by Christian writers themselves concerning the Church in India. However, earlier accounts do exist of the arrival of the faith in the country: one concerns Thomas the Apostle; another relates to the Christians from East Syria reaching the southwest coast of India between the second and third centuries CE.

The tradition current among the St. Thomas Christians in India is that he is believed to have landed on the southwest coast of India in about 52CE, before proceeding around the tip of India up the east coast to the ancient settlement of Mylapore, now a part of Chennai (Madras). He appears to have been killed there in approximately 72CE. Several Syrian Christian Churches that exist in this region claim to have been established by him. There is no contesting account of either the life of St. Thomas or of Christianity in India, rendering this claim possible; and indeed, the area around Chennai is rich in association with him. Thomas is thought to have lived in Saidapet, today a bustling part of the city. Most famously, the place where he died, now called St. Thomas Mount, has always been linked to him. But undoubtedly, the Portuguese, who controlled this area in the early sixteenth century, reinforced the connection; when not destroying Hindu temples, they were building churches and generally asserting Christianity in a quite forceful manner.

In the long period between Thomas and the coming of the European powers, the small but secure Syrian Christian community continued to exist in the midst of the ancient culture in which it found itself. Neither converting others nor losing its identity, it kept or adopted practices that are now thought of as specifically Hindu, such as the tying of a sacred necklace on the bride at marriage.

RIGHT Commissioned during the reign of Jahangir (1605–1627), this Mughal work known as *The Deposition from the Cross* is said to have been inspired by Flemish prints of European Renaissance art which reached the Mughal court. Just a few decades earlier a Jesuit mission had visited Fatehpur Sikri to try to convert Akbar. Jesus' Descent from the Cross is a key moment in the Christian faith – the Mughal representation captures the full torment of the horrific scene: Jesus' body is shown being lowered from the Cross, while at its base is a group of mourners who include the Virgin and Mary Magdalene.

THE FORMS
OF THE DIVINE

LEFT The narratives of
Vishnu as the supreme,
loving and gracious god of
blessings (*bhagavan*), who
comes down to Earth at
times of crisis to save the
world, were composed in a
series of devotional
Puranas, the *Hari Vamsa* and
the *Bhagavata Purana* being
the most influential. Vishnu
is depicted in this 18th-
century painting with his
consort Lakshmi, goddess
of wealth and prosperity,
flying to the aid of humans
on the back of the eagle
Garuda. As well as acting as
Vishnu's divine mount, the
valorous Garuda was a
destroyer of evil and
protector of humankind.

From spirit mothers who bless childless women to an all-powerful God who assumes fantastic forms to establish order on Earth, from animal envoys of good fortune to the ineffable principle of being that grounds all reality, the Hindu tradition encompasses a staggering profusion of ideas of the divine, as evident from the very earliest texts. Rather than succeeding developments stamping out the older belief systems, they came to co-exist, with different ideas serving different needs. With the exception of the concept of the ultimate (*brahman*), in Hinduism all divinity is understood through vivid forms. God possesses many qualities and assumes many aspects – these are realized in glorious detail in order to bring them closer to the human vision of the divine.

BELOW An 18th-century
carved ivory relief from
Madurai showing the
marriage of Shiva and
Parvati. Together with their
children (the warrior god
Skanda and the elephant-
headed Ganesha), they are
referred to as the "divine
family"(see page 107).

HINDUISM

The words "Hindu" and "India" are both derived from the Sanskrit "Sindhu", meaning Indus River. The term "Hinduism" itself is somewhat nebulous. It referred initially to those who lived beyond the river. Muslims revived the word's usage when they first came to India – their name for the country was Hindustan, "the place of Hindus". It was the Europeans who, in their attempt to analyze and catalogue the cultures of the world they were conquering, used the word "Hinduism" as a single term for all the inter-related beliefs and practices they found amongst the people called "Hindu". To complicate matters further, despite their distinctiveness, Buddhism, Jainism and Sikhism share many different beliefs and practices with Hindus. Indeed, in India, even Muslim and Christian practices overlap with Hindu ones.

One of Hinduism's chief characteristics is its tremendous variety of regional and local manifestations. Common texts, deities, traditions and patterns of ritual can be shared extensively, but interpreted differently. While certain broad threads can be traced across thousands of years, there appears to be both a Hindu tradition and simultaneously many Hindu traditions. The word "tradition" is particularly significant in its indication of the fact that Hinduism is a religion, a culture and a way of life in which there are no clear boundaries between the sacred and other spheres. Some texts and practices concern themselves with the path to liberation from the cycle of life, death and rebirth, while others reflect a desire to enhance the quality of life on Earth through singing, dancing, healing, astrology, sculpture and architecture; still others are concerned with ethical conduct.

The earliest textual beliefs concerning the divine are found in the *Veda*s (ca. 1500–1100BCE), a collection of sacred books on ritual activity for the maintenance of cosmic order (see page 54). The *Veda*s talk of the *devas* ("gods", ultimately akin to

div, meaning "light", and to the English "divine"), who personify various cosmic forces: Indra, their king, symbolizes thunder; Varuna, another regal figure, rain; Agni, often the most significant for his role in ritual, is fire; Surya, the sun; Chandra, the moon; Ushas, the female deity of dawn; Ratri, night, and so on. Among the most abstract is Vach, the female deity of speech. Different hymns praise different deities as supreme, a practice known as henotheism.

The significance of these deities lay in the fact that they represented cosmic forces: offering sacrifices to them was believed to maintain order and prosperity. But the priests who performed these rituals eventually became more important than the Vedic deities themselves, who never regained their former greatness. An altogether different and intellectual idea of reality and its meaning arose, centred on the abstract concept of *brahman* (see pages 8 and 128). Popular religion began increasingly to focus on gods who had been minor figures in the *Veda*s but were now taking on far more significant theological characteristics: this was particularly true of the gods Vishnu, Shiva and the Devi.

LEFT **The Hindu tradition has long acknowledged the sanctity of nature, with each of the major natural forces – including rain, thunder, wind, fire, the sun and the moon – being assigned a particular deity (see pages 42–43). This 9th–10th-century black shale sculpture from Bihar, eastern India, is of Surya, the Hindu god of the sun, whose temples are to be found throughout the country. A benevolent deity, he is believed to have the power to heal the sick – the placing of a sun symbol over a house or shop is thought to bring good fortune to its inhabitants. Although a relatively minor deity, Surya is invoked by Hindus in daily prayers.**

THE INCARNATIONS OF VISHNU

BELOW A 17th-century Rajput miniature depicting Vishnu's incarnation as the fish Matsya, who guided Manu, the first man, safely through a flood.

Initially Vishnu was a relatively minor deity in the *Rig Veda* (see page 54), an ally of the storm god Indra. From about the first century BCE, Vishnu grew in prominence – worshippers hailed him as the preserver of the universe, who pledged to come to Earth in animal or human form whenever ethical order (*dharma*) was threatened by selfishness or greed. His most notable divine quality was as the preserver who protects and sustains the world. By the second to the fifth century CE, many minor gods and the protagonists of hero narratives had been assimilated in his person by means of his *avatar*s – a word that is usually translated as "incarnations", but that refers more precisely to the number of times he descends to Earth to save the world – of which there were ten principal ones.

Vishnu's ten *avatar*s are as follows: as Matsya, the fish, he takes Manu, the first man, and the creatures of the world through a flood; as Kurma, the tortoise, he acts as the fulcrum for the churning of the cosmic ocean, in which the *deva*s (personifications of natural forces) gained the nectar of immortality; as Varaha, the boar, he rescues the Earth that has been cast into the cosmic ocean by a demon; as Narasimha, the hybrid man-lion, he protects an innocent boy-demon (this form was a favourite of many Hindu kings, because of its combination of grace and power); as Vamana, the Dwarf, he outwits another demon-king, who laughingly grants him the right to three steps of land only to have

Vishnu regain his cosmic form and occupy all heaven and Earth (in this story, the
ethically complex issue of a generous demon is explored, as he keeps his promise
and offers his own head as the third step he had granted); as Parasurama he plays an
ambiguous role, a *brahmin* (priest) who takes up the axe to wipe out the warrior
class (*kshatriya*) for their murder of his mother (this story clearly speaks of the ideo-
logical battle between priests and warriors for supreme status in society). Vishnu's
seventh and ninth *avatar*s as Rama and Krishna are the most popular by far (see
pages 102 and 103). In the traditional versions, the eighth is somewhat problematic:
it appears that Vishnu was both Balarama and his younger brother, Krishna; each
kills a different demon, but the two *avatar*s then co-exist. Medieval and modern

versions solve this problem and astonishingly give the Buddha as the ninth *avatar*, incorporating the great founder of another religion into Hinduism. The tenth *avatar* will be Kalki, who will ride on a white horse and usher in the end of this present cycle of time.

The story of Rama in the *Ramayana* ("The Wanderings of Rama", see pages 56 and 59) appears to have developed separately from the worship of Vishnu. The epic poem tells of Rama, prince of Ayodhya, who won the hand of Princess Sita. Banished to the forest through the trickery of his stepmother (whose own son was utterly loyal to Rama), he lives in happy solitude with Sita and his brother Laksmana. When Sita is kidnapped by the demon-king Ravana of Lanka, the brothers are assisted by the monkey-king Sugriva and his lieutenant Hanuman. The monkey army joins Rama in crossing the sea to Lanka, where he defeats and kills Ravana; the period of banishment over, he returns to Ayodhya. The normative picture of Rama is at his coronation, accompanied by his wife, brothers and Hanuman. Rama and Sita are both exemplars for the tradition, although the interpretations of their actions have changed with circumstances. The tale shows no sign of Rama's divinity, but the tradition

LEFT **A 12th-century copper statue from Madurai of Ramachandra, the eponymous hero of the *Ramayana*. Although cast in the capital city of the Pandya kingdom, it follows the innovative style of the bronze sculptures of the Chola empire (see pages 80–81).**

—102—

generally recognizes them as Vishnu and his consort Lakshmi deliberately taking human form in order to guide people.

The story of Krishna tells how Vishnu once again took bodily form, this time to defeat the wicked Kamsa, his uncle who had usurped the throne from Krishna's grandfather. The character appears to be a fusion of a deified princely hero of the North and a local or tribal Indian flute-playing forest god. On a stormy night, Krishna is born to Kamsa's sister Devaki and her husband Vasudeva. Kamsa wants to kill the baby, but Vasudeva smuggles him away to the countryside, where he is raised by the cowherd Nanda and his wife Yashoda. His childhood is full of mischief, but there are also intimations of his divinity: when scolded by his mother for putting mud in his mouth, he opens it to reveal the universe to her. At this point, Krishna entrances the *gopi*s, the cowherd women. His favourite is the beautiful Radha. The pining of Radha and her fellow *gopi*s for Krishna, their magical intimacy and his abandonment of them in the course of his long earthly life are understood to represent an image of the soul's longing for and intermittent experience of God. Krishna eventually kills the evil Kamsa. At a much later period in his life, in the great war between the Pandavas and Kauravas depicted in the epic text the *Mahabharata* (see pages 56–58), Krishna is the enigmatic cousin of the sons of the rival families, and does not fight on either side. He offers the two sides a choice between his personal service and the use of his army. The ethical Pandavas choose him and he becomes the charioteer of the Pandava prince Arjuna. In the *Bhagavad Gita* (see pages 56–58), which is set on the eve of the battle which the Pandavas win at great cost, he teaches Arjuna the way to a fulfilling spiritual life before revealing himself as God.

DANCING FOR THE DIVINITIES

Dance has always been a potent and highly sacred art-form in India. The *Natya Shastra*, the classical text revealed to the sage Bharata (ca. 200BCE), lays down precise rules for the formal display of the pure expression of essential human emotions (drama) and of the narration of stories. For some two thousand years an elaborate discipline of dance was based on this text, and consequently became known as *Bharata natyam* ("the dance of Bharata") – the tradition survived in the performances of the South Indian female temple dancers (*devadasi*s, or "servants of the gods"). Although its practice has fluctuated at various times in recent centuries, *Bharata natyam* is today a popular but nevertheless still rigorous discipline, and is the best-known form of classical dance in India.

The temple dance of South India seeks to embody both the human response to the divine and the representation of the divine itself. Some dances tell of forlorn young women yearning for their lovers – as in the case of the female cowherds (*gopi*s) pining for the absent Krishna (see page 103); other dances symbolize Shiva's various cosmic moods as the lord of the dance (Nataraja; see pages 36–37). For dancer (pictured, right), musical accompanist and audience alike, dance is the means by which tales of the human love for the divine and the divine's miraculous interventions in human life can be enacted at religious and social ceremonies and celebrations, such as weddings and births. In these various contexts, dance acts as a sacred ritual, a deeply symbolic form of worship in which the dancers are thought to entice blessings from the gods.

THE CREATOR AND DESTROYER

BELOW Ganesha, the elephant-headed son of Shiva and Parvati, is one of India's most important deities. As remover of obstacles and lord of beginnings he is often invoked by Hindus before embarking on business ventures, tasks or journeys. He is shown in this 18th-century painting detail in characteristically benevolent guise.

Shiva – embodiment of opposites, creator and destroyer, lover and ascetic yogi, husband and hermit – was worshipped in many forms and represents parts of the cyclical cosmic process of creation, sustenance, destruction and re-creation, a creative potency. He has five main aspects. The first is as an aloof meditating ascetic on Mount Kailasa who generates the religious power to sustain the entire universe (see pages 40 and 53). His second main form is as Nataraja, the divine dancer whose joyous movements are those of life itself – sometimes peaceful, sometimes fervent (see page 36). The dance eases his devotees' suffering, but is also the *tandava* dance of destruction that returns the universe to chaos at the close of each age.

In the form of Bhairava, Shiva is a destroyer of demons. He is also Buteshvara, lord of ghosts, wearing human skulls and writhing garlands of snakes while he dances in cremation grounds. His fourth aspect is as a powerful fertility god, worshipped in the aniconic form of the phallus (*linga*) and linked to fertility symbols such as the crescent moon, bulls and snakes. He is also the divine male, creating the world with the feminine embodiment of his power *shakti* (Sanskrit, *sakti*), his consort Parvati. In his fifth aspect, he is a benevolent god of medicine, a lord of healing herbs. In his protective aspect he used his hair to break the fall of the Ganges River when it flowed from heaven (see illustration, page 42).

These often contradictory aspects derived from Shiva having assimilated a number of gods. For example, from his antecedents in the Indus civilization he apparently took his qualities as a fertility god and as yogic lord of meditation – he is often represented in deep concentration and in different yogic postures (see illustration, page 53). From the Vedic god Rudra, Shiva received his combined aspect as creator-destroyer and his role as god of medicine.

But these features also reflected the ancient Indian capacity to see opposites combined and transformed in one being – as male and female were united in Shiva's and Parvati's androgynous combination, Ardhanarishvara (see page 12). Shiva is an ambivalent figure and manifests the extremes of asceticism and eroticism – he is often depicted in meditation with an erection, and his tremendous sexual control enabled him to make love for hundreds of years to his consort Parvati. Paradoxically, Shiva is only definable by means of the oppositions that he embodies. His divine family includes his children Skanda, a warrior god, and the elephant-headed Ganesha, the remover of obstacles. Skanda was early on identified with Murugan, the Tamil god of the hills, an association that strengthened the presence of Shiva in southern Indian culture. Ganesha – known by a variety of names – quickly became one of the most influential mediating figures in popular religion, invoked at the start of every venture.

RIGHT **A sandstone figure, ca. 400CE, of Shiva from the Mathura region of Uttar Pradesh. In this form he is both the aniconic *linga*, the symbol of creative and erotic potency, and the iconic ascetic. When opened, his third eye – here closed in tranquillity – will burn up the world so that it can be created anew.**

THE GODDESS

Worship of the Mother Goddess can be traced back to the dawn of civilization in ancient India, although by the time of the sacrificial religion of the early Vedic period, She was less celebrated. The fundamental theological claim of the sacred text the *Devi Mahatmyam* (first to second century CE) was that the divine, in its true and original form, is female. This divinity, known as Devi, gives birth to the universe, including the male deities; she herself then takes the form of a young

woman, but draws upon the male deities' combined power to destroy evil. This narrative of the Devi claimed that the consorts of male deities were to be understood as simply so many forms of her. However, the traditional male-oriented narratives sought to dilute this perspective (see also caption, left).

Lakshmi or Shri was the consort of Vishnu. She took many forms to be with him through his series of incarnations: these ranged from Padma to Princess Sita and Radha, Krishna's beloved *gopi* (see page 103). Lakshmi was generally represented with the full breasts and wide hips of a fertility goddess, standing or seated on a lotus, attended by a white owl and bathed in water poured from the trunks of devout elephants. Her worshippers praised her as goddess of wealth and prosperity.

Shiva's consort and wife represents a successful assimilation of the Devi cult. As Sati, she threw herself into a fire, angered at her father's disregard for her husband. Shiva was distraught and embarked on a tender and mournful dance through the world with his beloved's body in his arms. He then entered a state of perfect meditation. Sati was reborn as Parvati, who won Shiva through her determined devotion. Parvati was seen as both gentle Uma and as fearsome black-skinned Durga, spouse of Shiva in his aspect as Bhairava, destroyer of demons. From Durga's forehead emerged another terrifying incarnation of the Goddess: Kali, who was renowned for her bloodthirstiness yet revered as the Mother (see page 110).

Sarasvati was the patroness of music, poetry and scriptures; generally she was represented holding a lyre (the *vina*), sitting on a rock or riding a white swan. In medieval times, she came to be seen as the consort of Brahma, the creator god.

The feminine principle was played out endlessly, and numerous female local spirits and guardian deities came over time to be associated with the Devi.

LEFT **Seven goddess figures – the Saptamatrika – are represented in this 10th-century relief from central India. All except one derive their names and attributes from their male consorts. According to the text the *Devi Mahatmyam*, the male deities could function only through the *shakti* (power) that the corresponding goddesses embodied. More male-oriented narratives sought to contain this perception of feminine power. The end figure (far left) in this lintel is probably Shiva. From (second) left to near right, the goddesses are Maheshvari, Brahmani, Kaumari, Vaishnavi, Varahi, Indrani and Chamundi.**

FEARSOME FEMALES: DURGA AND KALI

The mighty goddess Durga, a manifestation of the Devi and a slayer of demons, is best known for her annihilation of the buffalo-demon Mahishasura. Durga is shown here (right, in an early 13th-century sculpture), composed and serene following the gruesome battle, with the weapons of war in her hands. From her forehead emerged Kali (Sanskrit for "black"). This fearsome progeny, a symbol of Durga's anger, was renowned for her bloodthirstiness: on slaying the demon Raktavija, she held him above her head and drank all his blood. Common aspects of her depiction are a black body, a bloodstained mouth, a red protruding tongue and the wearing or carrying of human skulls (see above, and left and right). Despite her ferocity she came to be revered as the Mother – fierce but also fiercely loving of her devotees.

THE HOLY GANGES

The sun sets on the mighty river Ganges (Sanskrit, Ganga), silhouetting Varanasi (right, also known as Benares), the most important city on its 1,560-mile (2,510km) journey through India. The holiest of all the country's revered waterways, the Ganges has six other sacred cities located along its route, including Allahabad, where the river has a confluence with two others – the Yamuna and the mythical Sarasvati (see page 43). The literal as well as mythological power and importance of the holy river Ganges to the people of India is immense: bathing in its waters is said to purify the spirit, while dying in the cities on its banks brings liberation from the cycle of lives.

In Hindu belief the Ganges is associated with the goddess Ganga and, according to myth, the sage Bhargava underwent extreme austerities to bring the divine Ganga down to Earth in order to cleanse the impurities of his impious ancestors. Delighted by his devotion, the goddess came rushing down with such force that her crashing waters threatened to cause devastation on Earth. But the god Shiva, meditating on Mount Kailasa (see page 40), cushioned her fall by catching her in his matted hair and knotting it up until the terrible flow subsided. As the earthly manifestation of the goddess, the river's heavenly purity was thereafter believed to wash away the sins of all who bathe in her. This story of the great river's heavenly origin is celebrated in the annual festival of Ganga Dussera.

The actual source of the river is a rock-face called Gomukhi (The Face of the Cow), located high in the Himalayas, near Gangotri. From there it proceeds down through the plains of North India until it eventually empties into the Bay of Bengal. Historically, the waters of the river nourished the heart of ancient Indian culture, which explains the many references to it in some of the key texts and narratives of Hinduism.

DEMIGODS AND SPIRITS

A rich variety of hybrid creatures, animal spirits and demigods inhabited the myths and adorned the temples of ancient India. In heaven, they interacted with and assisted the gods in many different ways: some gave support in battle, others provided entertainment during less troubled times. On Earth, too, they were believed to play important roles – for example, as temple protectors or bringers of fertility. Dwarf-like spirits called *gana*s were thought to have the power to protect temples against evil or negative spiritual forces and their images were carved on the temple surfaces. The *gana*s were protected by the god Shiva and commanded by Ganesha, who was known as the lord of the *gana*s. They were originally nature spirits, probably honoured alongside Shiva's antecedent, the Indus civilization's lord of beasts.

*Gana*s were assisted in protecting temples by *vyala*s and *yali*s – these were terrifying and often hideous hybrid creatures that combined the powerful body of a lion with the fearsome head of an elephant, tiger, or bird. They were depicted with eyes bulging, just at the point of triumphing over an enemy.

Other celebrated hybrids were the half-human, half-snake *naga*s, guardians of treasure and esoteric

LEFT **A carved wooden** *dvarapala* **or "guardian of the gate", ca. 12th–13th century, from Kerala, southwest India. With their bulging eyes and ferocious aspect, these protector spirits were often positioned outside temples dedicated to Vishnu to ward off negative forces and unwelcome visitors.**

writings, and denizens of the underworld kingdom of Nagaloka. Their princesses were known for their astonishing beauty, and certain royal houses, including the Pallava dynasty of southern India, claimed their origin in the ancient marriage of a human king and a *naga* queen. *Naga*s possessed considerable symbolic power and were associated with seas, rivers, streams and wells. On temples they were shown adopting a reverent posture in the presence of the major gods and goddesses.

Vishnu temples often had fierce-faced "guardians of the gate" (*dvarapala*s) carved on the doorposts of shrines. "Divine beauties" (*surasundari*s) were sometimes shown with a bird or a monkey or performing their ablutions. These heavenly maidens — with the wide hips, tiny waists, and swelling breasts of fertility goddesses — were one of many groups of voluptuous and graceful spirit-women praised by ancient Indians. Another group was the *apsara*s, lithe dancing maidens who added visible beauty to the songs of the heavenly singers and instrumentalists known as the *gandharva*s, who endowed humankind with the gift of music.

In the *Mahabharata* (see pages 56–58), the *gandharva*s and *apsara*s entertained their divine masters with song and dance in the heavenly halls and gardens laid out by the divine craftsman Tvastr. *Apsara*s played key roles in many narratives and were often sent from heaven to captivate heroes with their beauty or to distract meditating sages whose powers were feared.

*Yakshi*s were female fertility spirits, bringers of abundance, and sometimes associated with trees and other natural phenomena. Carvings of these benevolent spirits survive from the second century BCE. *Yakshi*s had their male counterparts in *yaksha*s and it is thought that both were possible ancestors of the guardian spirits — *dvarapala*s and *surasundari*s — that were later carved on stone temples.

FORCES OF IGNORANCE

The opponents of righteousness and the representatives of doubt and ignorance were known as *asuras*. These demon figures were brothers of the gods, members of an extended divine family who had degenerated. They represent cosmic disorder, and their defeat is always a sign that the cosmos is running smoothly.

The demons had narrowly missed out on immortality at the time of the churning of the ocean of milk. On Vishnu's instructions, gods and demons shared the labour of churning the great ocean in order to bring forth the divine drink *amrita*, which made all those who drank it immortal. When the gods' physician Dhanwantari arose from the ocean holding a cup of *amrita*, the demons seized it, but before they could consume it Vishnu took it back. The gods happily drank down the *amrita*, and thereafter could never die or be killed. However, the demon Rahu disguised himself as a god and managed to taste the precious drink. The gods tried to kill him, but the *amrita* had made his head and neck immortal: Rahu rose into the sky, where at times of eclipse he gains a measure of revenge against the gods by swallowing the sun and moon. Because they were denied the chance to drink *amrita*, none of the other *asuras* could cheat death forever in this way, although from time to time individual demons generated so much *tapas* (inner heat) through austerities that Brahma was forced to make them invulnerable for a particular time or according to agreed conditions.

Although persistent foes of the gods, demons were not irredeemably wicked, for in the ancient Indian understanding, there was no pure evil, only evil manifested as a sign of psychological and cosmic disorder. The root of wicked conduct was ignorance or a lack of understanding of the nature of goodness and order. Hence, knowledge was the key to overcoming the darkness of mind and spirit.

RIGHT This menacing detail, from an 18th-century image attributed to the famous Indian Pahari painter Nainsukh, conjures up the powerfully oppressive forces of darkness that were associated with demonic and dangerous beings such as the *asuras*. Although not irredeemably evil, these figures were greatly feared as disrupters of ritual. On occasion they were also shown to be equal to, if not more mighty than, the gods themselves, forcing the latter to retreat temporarily when confronted by their awesome power.

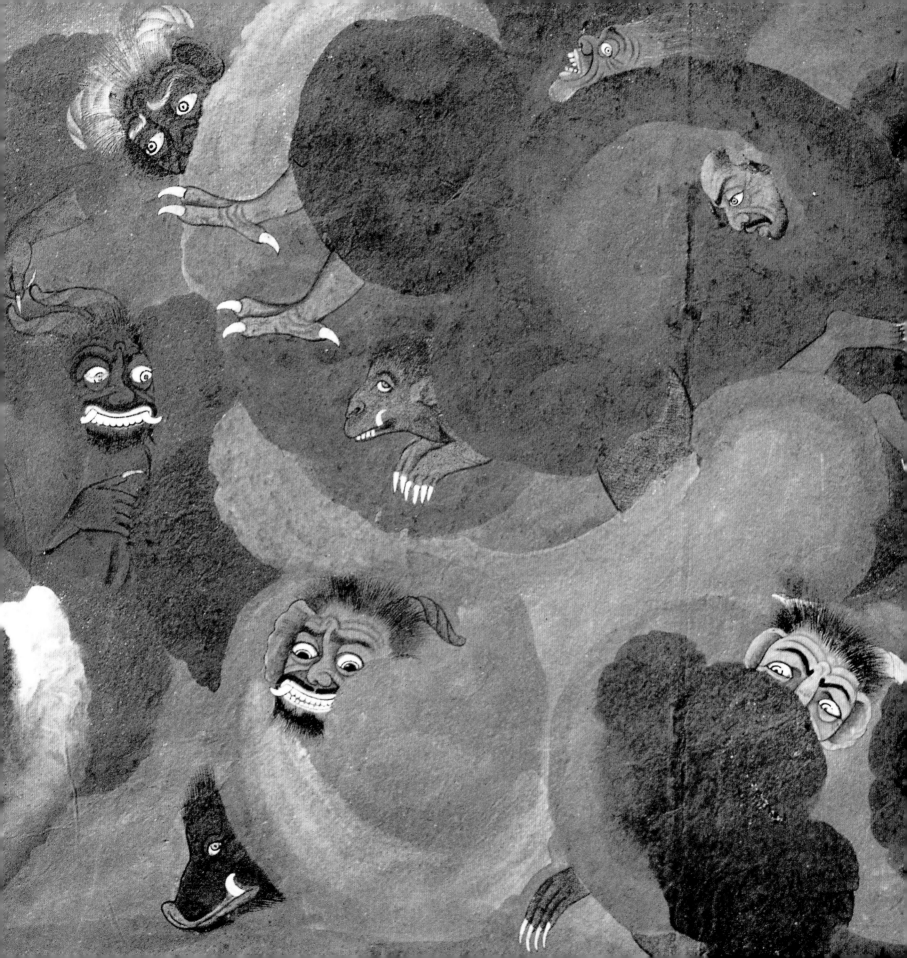

THE SPIRIT OF INQUIRY

LEFT An early 19th-century Indian chart depicting southern and northern hemisphere constellations, using Roman-derived patterns. Astrological knowledge was highly prized in India and great importance was attached to horoscopes, which were cast at birth and consulted regularly to determine the most auspicious times on which to conduct the important events in an individual's life, such as marriage or a new business venture. The skills required to observe and calculate the movements of the heavens played a significant part in the development of mathematics. The eminent mathematician Bhaskara (see pages 130–131) was himself from a family of royal astrologers.

Ancient India's highly developed sense of order and its fluid, dynamic and creative culture contributed to its longevity in the face of major internal and external political changes. Although, to some extent, these factors were in tension with each other, its sense of order created a stable world for intellectual activity that was able to withstand invasions, imperial collapse and shifting political power. Many notable intellectual achievements were tied to religion, and this relationship tells us much about life in the ancient land. Theories on language, knowledge, mind and logic evolved within the search for liberation; arithmetical and geometric techniques were developed for use in the performance and timing of rituals; and medical science sought to integrate spiritual and physical wellbeing.

BELOW The object contained in this ornate gold case is a "Goa stone" – an amalgam of cure-all herbal remedies condensed into a hard ball. These balls were man-made versions of the calcified concentrations, known as *bezoar*, found in the stomachs of some animals and highly prized for their medicinal properties.

ORDER AND FREEDOM

The ideal organization of Indian society was put forward in the *Purusa Sukta* ("Hymn to the Cosmic Person"), a hymn in the *Rig Veda*. The model appears to have been an attempt to make sense of the changing and already pluralistic society of the Vedic people, although scholars differ as to its exact meaning. In the hymn, the Cosmic Person is offered as a sacrifice to itself by the gods. "His mouth became the *brahmin* [priest], his hands were made into the *kshatriya* [the warrior], his thighs became the *vaisya*s [merchants], and from his feet were born the *sudra*s [the servants]. The moon was born from his mind; the sun was born from his eye … from his breath was born the wind … from his head the sky … Thus the gods ordered the world." The concept of order is articulated as natural: the social classes are as much a part of the structure of the cosmos as natural phenomena and celestial bodies. The division of society was therefore a powerful concept from very early times.

The four classes (*varna*) became hereditary over the centuries. This religiously sanctioned idea of differentiated society was used to legitimize the subsequent assignation of groups to one or another class. But the hierarchy was always subject to pressures. The warrior and merchant classes often had cause to challenge the priestly control of sacred knowledge; at the same time, priests and warriors joined to assimilate religious movements that contested their authority. Moreover, the real identification of people was not with a class but with local communities or castes (*jati*), whose solidarity lay in inter-marriage, common myths of origin, religious practices, and so on. Each *jati* would belong to a *varna*, although in different parts of India this could vary: a group that was *sudra* in one place might be *vaisya* in another.

The status of individual *jati*s constantly shifted as occupations and circumstances changed, allowing for some mobility for all but the most marginal and

BELOW A painting, ca. 1828, of a Hindu marriage procession. According to the division of ancient Indian society, individuals had to marry partners from the same *jati* or caste and to adhere to the ceremonial practices associated specifically with that caste.

despised groups that were not part of the caste system. Periodically, there would be movements that sought to deny such fundamental difference, from Buddhism and Jainism to the poets of *bhakti* (devotionalism) who argued for the equality of all. But people often sought social status as groups rather than as individuals, and the traditional divisions were re-emphasized, albeit with constantly changing status.

All civilizations generate their ideas and achievements through their elites; in the case of ancient India, it was predominantly through the activities of *brahmin*s, whose intellectual dominance remained untouched.

THE RISE OF TECHNOLOGY

The cities of the Indus culture show that by 2500BCE there was competence in street planning, building and drainage; but these skills appear to have been lost, re-emerging only in the later urbanization of North India (500BCE–500CE). The Indus culture had also mastered the technique of smelting bronze and copper, with fine bronze drills being a notable achievement. The *Vedas* even mention tin coating for copper vessels.

We have little knowledge of the early architectural techniques of this period because buildings were built out of wood, but foreign descriptions of the Maurya capital at Pataliputra (see pages 76–77) point to a thriving city. Stone buildings, initially Buddhist monasteries and

LEFT Metallurgy, closely linked to chemistry, was among the Indians' most ancient sciences. There is evidence that the use of bronze and other metals was an important and distinctive feature of the life of the early culture of the Indus Valley (see page 14). The magnificent bronze elephant with a seated *mahout*, or elephant driver, shown here (12th–13th century) is from Tamil Nadu and is a fine example of the exceptional skill and inventiveness of the early Indian metalworkers.

*stupa*s (reliquary mounds), not only required building techniques (probably learnt from Mesapotamia) but also effective metal tools.

By the fourth century BCE, there was considerable awareness of metallurgy and iron began to be handled. The most majestic example of ancient Indian metallurgical skills is the fifth-century Delhi Iron Pillar. Of virtually pure iron, even today it shows no sign of rust. Iron-casting technology was such that in the tenth to the twelfth centuries, temples such as those at Puri and Konarak were using iron beams and girders then unmatched anywhere in the world for their size. High-quality steel was also produced from around the sixteenth century.

Irrigation had been used extensively even in the Indus culture (see page 14) and the great empires of India relied heavily on the system. By the tenth to the eleventh centuries, in both North and South India, water management included the construction of reservoirs and massive artificial lakes.

Classical Indian theories relating to the spiritual and psychological symbolism of colours fed into treatises that influenced the development of textile dyeing. Textile technology, using complex manual machinery, flourished from an early time, allowing Indian kingdoms to run massive trade surpluses against Rome and succeeding European societies. Other areas of skilled manufacture included carpet-weaving, metalwork, jewellery and stone carving. Glass took a long time to come to India, largely as a result of the lack of demand for windows in a hot climate.

A complex set of social and geographic conditions, combined with a tendency to view technology as irrelevant to spiritual, philosophical and cultural aspirations, halted the progress of Indian technology in the fifteenth to the seventeenth centuries, ruling out the possibility of a native Indian Industrial Revolution.

THE ART AND SCIENCE OF HEALING

The Indian medical tradition is full of lost works, but the medical encyclopedias written by Caraka, Susruta and Bhela (first century BCE to the first century CE), which are the most authoritative and influential, have survived. Their sophistication and comprehensiveness indicate that they belonged to a tradition that must have been flourishing for many centuries previously. There is as yet no clear evidence on the origins of this tradition, known as *ayurveda* ("the science of health"), although some of the palliative practices in the Buddhist monasteries in the third to the second centuries BCE must have contributed to them.

The medical systems developed by the physicians Caraka and Susruta appear to have been highly developed and high-status ones. Their texts were in Sanskrit, drawing on the philosophical learning of the day, and the physicians (*vaidya*) were honoured members of society. Upon completion of their apprenticeship, according to Caraka, physicians should hear a sermon from their teacher, which included such guidance as: "When you go to the home of the patient, you should direct your words, mind, intellect and senses to your patient. Nothing that happens in the house of the patient must be discussed outside, nor must the patient's condition be reported to anyone who might harm the patient." These guidelines functioned very much like the Hippocratic Oath of Greece.

Ayurveda had an elaborate account of the metabolic process, and a typology of the body based on fluids and "humours". While the balance of the humours (wind, bile and phlegm) was thought to explain good health, the ancient doctors did not content themselves with treating illness as merely an imbalance in the humours. They sought to give a more detailed account of the origin of diseases. The

"abandonment of good sense" through lack of intelligence, will-power or memory, was a significant source of illness, as was the suppression of natural urges (that is, excluding bad deeds) relating to excretion, sex, wind, nausea, yawning, and hunger. But the effect of past actions (*karma*) and demonic possession were also postulated as causes of illness. Adherence to sensible diagnostic procedures – touching, looking and questioning – was stipulated within the tradition.

The two most important areas of medical achievement in ancient Indian medicine were in surgery and pharmacology. Surgery was part of the physician's work, unlike in Europe. Caesarean sections, the removal of gall-bladders, lancing of boils, reduction of dislocations and suturing of wounds were among the most highly developed procedures. But the most striking skills were in rhinoplasty (which until the nineteenth century was more advanced than in Europe) and in plastic surgery to correct hare-lips. In pharmacology, thousands of plants formed the basis of medicines and were described in an elaborate typology.

ABOVE **A late 18th-century illustration shows a surgeon or *jarrah* swabbing the leg of a patient following the treatment of a wound. There is a clear indication that the anaesthetic used in the procedure was opium – this would doubtless have been one of the most effective of the limited choices available at that time. Surgery was one of the eight branches of *ayurveda*, and was an area of medical science in which tremendous advances were made in ancient India.**

WHEELS OF POTENCY

*Chakra*s ("wheels") are energy centres at which the body's *nadi*s, or subtle nerve channels, intersect and through which *prana* flows. Located along the spine, the seven *chakra*s are associated with specific functions and symbolic elements and colours – for example, the one in the neck region, *vishuddha* (above), is sixteen-petalled and bluish – and they are often represented as discs on the body, as shown in this eighteenth-century painting (right). Coiled up in the root *chakra*, the *muladhara*, near the anus, lies the fabled *kundalini shakti* (symbolized by the snake, left and right), the primal energy that can be channelled through the body to the *sahasrara chakra* (at the crown), which contains the divine presence. Practices such as yoga help the free flow of *prana* to facilitate good physical and emotional health.

KNOWLEDGE AND LIBERATION

RIGHT **This colossal statue (57 feet/18m) of the Jain saint Gommateshvara stands at the summit of Indragiri Hill at Shravana Belgola, southern India, and was completed in the late 10th century. Gommateshvara defeated his brother in the struggle to succeed their late father. With victory secured, he then acknowledged the futility of conflict by giving the kingdom to his brother, renouncing the world and seeking enlightenment. The ant hill built around him and the creepers and snakes entwining his limbs symbolize the depth of his meditative state. Gommateshvara's story is indicative of the significant impact that the Jain and Buddhist philosophical traditions (and in particular their quest for meaning and for knowledge of the world) had on the development of spiritual and intellectual life in ancient India.**

In the *Rig Veda*'s "Hymn of Creation", probing questions were asked about the nature of reality and the meaning of existence (see also pages 34–35). Similar complex themes were also later taken up in the *Upanishads* (see pages 54–55), texts that marked a major development in philosophical speculation as the sages strove to account for what they saw around them, in terms of some absolute principle of being (*brahman*) whose power and presence could explain everything (including the intimate presence of consciousness, through its pervasion of the self or *atman*).

The Buddha and Mahavira (see pages 62–66) brought an ethical urgency to the quest for meaning: they intuited that life was full of suffering, and sought ways to cleanse people of it. The Buddha inaugurated a long and significant tradition of reflective questioning, by stating that the very idea of some mysterious and unified self was an illusion. According to him, the desire that leads to suffering is caused by this illusion that there is a single self who desires things for itself; if the illusion is

exposed, there will be nothing to desire or to desire for. All people should be looked after and guided until they attain this realization. Mahavira accepted the reality of self, but claimed that suffering came through taking partial knowledge to be absolute; there are multiple sides to reality, and they all need to be understood, by extending sympathy to different beliefs. So, each in his way wanted his philosophical insights to result in compassion and tolerance. Later Hindu thought assimilated this ethical dimension into philosophy.

Inquiry into the nature of reality in ancient India was driven by the search for an ultimate state of being – a state free of suffering, free of rebirth, free of ethical and other blemishes. Knowing how things really are was believed to transform inquirers, making their consciousness pure and their conduct unsullied by selfishness. In this transformed state a person would attain freedom. This spiritual freedom was called *moksha* ("liberation", or "final release) or *nirvana* ("extinction"). It was this spiritual quest that provided the framework for philosophy.

However, once knowledge was sought, many directions of inquiry became possible: what is the nature of the physical world – does it really exist or do we create it in our minds?; what are the correct forms of reasoning through which we can arrive at settled conclusions?; how is consciousness possible?; how can it be transformed?; how do we gain knowledge of anything?; what are the means by which we gain knowledge?; if teaching and thinking require language, how does language become meaningful? These and numerous other sophisticated questions opened up over the centuries, and many different schools of thought (referred to as "ways of seeing" or *darsana*, the nearest equivalent to the Greek *philosophia* or "love of wisdom") grew up within Hindu, Buddhist and Jain traditions.

FROM ZERO TO INFINITY

Geometry evolved in ancient India through the need to provide layouts for ritual sites. Arithmetic developed quickly through the Vedic use of the decimal system. Mathematics proved successful because very early on, the Indians, unlike the Greeks, understood the concept of abstract numbers (and not just the numerical quantity of objects). They evolved such practices as raising numbers to the power of ten and manipulating them (so that, for example, 2×10^3 could be rewritten as 20×10^2) — ritual incantations, of course, consisted of arithmetical progressions. Many mathematical advances are seen in the *Sulbasutra*s (second century CE), texts on the preparation of rituals. They contained practical geometry and arithmetic as well as notable theories. *Sulba* mathematics includes transformations of geometric figures — square to circle, rectangle to square, square to isosceles trapezium, square to rhombus, circle to square — in which the areas are kept unchanged. Most notably, the *Sulbasutra*s have the oldest expression of the theorem commonly ascribed to the Greek mathematician Pythagoras (the sum of the areas of the squares on the two sides of a right-angled triangle is equal to that of its hypotenuse).

Several key concepts were born in ancient India. One was the theory of infinity, which was expressed philosophically in very early times and then proved later (in the seventh century) mathematically by Bhaskara. Another concept was that of zero and its symbolic value. (Bhaskara also proved that a number divided by zero was equal to zero.) Without these concepts modern mathematics would have been impossible. The so-called Arabic decimal system of numerals, that transformed European mathematics then trapped in the cumbersome Roman system, also originated in India. Unfortunately, the name of the mathematician who devised this extraordinarily significant system is unknown.

RIGHT Two leaves from Bhaskara's *Lilavati*, arguably the greatest work of this 12th-century mathematical genius and one which deals in detail with a range of mathematical operations (from division to square roots) and issues of geometry, such as the theorem of the square of the hypotenuse. The workings visible here (right) show calculations and diagrams relating to various problems involving right-angle triangles.

The most influential systematic mathematician after the author of the anonymous *Sulbasutra* texts, was Aryabhatta (born in 476CE). He provided rules for basic computation, geometric figures and numerical quantities. He also gave the modern approximate value of π (the unvarying ratio of the circumference of a circle to its diameter), which was far more accurate than that of the Greeks, expressed in the form 62832/20000; the mathematician Madhava took it to eleven decimal places.

By the thirteenth century, Indian mathematicians had anticipated the discoveries of the European Renaissance, including the import of positive and negative quantities, the systems for extracting square roots and cube roots, and solutions for certain indeterminate equations. And in the fifteenth century, Madhava discovered a variety of trigonometric functions.

STUDYING THE HEAVENS

The origins of Indian astronomy lay in the effort to determine the correct time for the performance of Vedic rituals. Astronomy was called "The Auxiliary of the *Veda*s, On [Sky-] Light" (*jyotisa vedanga*) and the earliest astronomical texts date to between the fifth and the third centuries BCE. The calendar that was used to fix the dates for rituals, which shows signs of Mesapotamian influence, was not entirely accurate. The heavens were divided into 27 or 28 sections that were named according to the groups of stars (*naksatra*) on the ecliptic or apparent orbit of the sun, near which the moon passes on each day of its cycle.

Around the first century CE, there was a short and revolutionary period of Hellenic influence; the sixth century text of the Indian astronomer, philosopher and mathematician Varahamihira mentions the Roman School and the Pauline School (named after the astronomer Paul of Alexandra). Indian astronomical constants, on the basis of which calendrical calculations were made, were much improved by the adoption of geometrical models, the signs of the zodiac, the seven-day week, and the hour. But very quickly, Indian

LEFT A bronze celestial sphere from the mid-17th century. As early as the 6th century, the Indian astronomer–mathematician Aryabhatta proposed that the Earth was round and that it rotated on its axis. Among the many various objections to the theory of the Earth's rotation were that if this were so, then clothes on a line would fly; the falcon, which rises high in the sky, would be unable to find its way back; the tops of trees would be destroyed; and the ocean would invade the land.

astronomy drew on its much more advanced mathematics to build an astronomy that, through the Arab caliphs of Baghdad (who employed Indian astronomers), passed back to Europe between the ninth and the thirteenth centuries.

In the sixth century, the mathematician–astronomer Aryabhatta (see also caption, left) observed that what people had perceived previously as the apparent rotation of the planets was actually the "rotation of the Earth on its axis"; this was a tremendous insight at a time when Europe believed in a flat Earth. But astronomically speaking, the Indians were also geocentric, and astronomical practice was therefore not affected by Aryabhatta's theory.

The Indians understood that the difference in behaviour between the outer planets visible to the naked eye and the inner ones was due to their different distances from Earth – an insight not grasped in Europe until the Renaissance. Again, the functional methods of the Indian astronomers were not affected by these theories, except in the great accuracy with which eclipses were predicted. Only much later did Nilakantha (1444–1542), unknown to the West, use these theories to develop a heliocentric model of the solar system (that is, with the sun not the Earth at its centre) at almost the same time as Tycho Brahe in Europe.

Ancient Indians had sought to predict the future through other forms of divination; it was only under Greek influence that significant predictive importance was attached to the celestial bodies (especially the Nine Planetary Gods, or *nava graha*: the seven observable planets and the ascending and descending nodes of the moon). The use of astronomy for prediction also led to the worship of the planets and the drawing up of astrological horoscopes based on an interpretation of planetary and stellar positions developed rapidly in the early centuries CE.

THE JANTAR MANTAR

Jai Singh II of Amber, the successor of Aurangzeb, was deeply interested in art and astronomy. He once observed a dispute between Hindu and Muslim astrologers concerning the auspicious time for the emperor to set out on an expedition and offered to clarify the astronomical data behind the dispute by building an observatory. The result was the construction in 1724 of the Jantar Mantar (literally, "Instrument and Formula") in Delhi.

The building's abstract structures are actually instruments – eighteen fixed ones in total – designed to track the times and movements of the sun, moon and planets, knowledge which, in part, enabled more accurate casting of horoscopes by astronomer–priests. One of the most striking objects is the Jai Prakash Yantra (shown here), a hemispherical two-bowl structure with a visible map of the heavens inscribed on the concave inner surface structures, with scales around the rim. It was built to reveal the zodiacal sign approaching the meridian, which was done by stretching cross-wires between cardinal points on the rim and watching the shadow of a ring (representing the sun) suspended from the cross-wire project the sun's position onto the structure and its celestial map.

Among the other instruments at Jantar Mantar are the "Prince of Dials" (Samrat Yantra); the Ram Yantra; and the Mishra Yantra, a pair of pillars used to determine the shortest and longest days of the year. The collection of instruments reflect the diversity of India's cultural influences: the use of platforms is reminiscent of Vedic fire altars; the architectural form is a Hindu–Islamic fusion; and the embodiment of order and unity is reminiscent of the mandala.

The Jantar Mantar was functional for just seven years due to political difficulties that overwhelmed the land. Jai Singh's dream of bringing practical astronomy to the people remained unfulfilled.

GLOSSARY

deva: a divine being (from a root word meaning "light"), conceived as having human form but representing a variety of natural forces (thunder, rain, fire) and abstract entities (language, mind); "gods" is an imperfect translation because they are not thought of as "real" beings except within mythic stories.

dharma: a complex word, most generally translated as "ethics". More specific concepts within ethics are also applicable depending on context, like an overarching cosmic order, appropriate conduct, and personal virtue.

moksha: liberation or release from the conditions of worldly existence.

naga: snake; a class of supernatural creatures associated with snakes.

nirvana: the Buddhist term for a condition beyond existence, literally meaning a "snuffing out" of the state of suffering.

samsara: the round of lives — birth, death and rebirth — that the impersonal being goes through until liberated.

TIMELINE

2600–1700BCE: Indus culture

1500–1100BCE: Period of the *Vedas*

1200–600BCE: Period of the *Brahmanas*, *Aranyaka*s and early *Upanishads*

ca. 599–527BCE: Life of Vardhamana Mahavira, the central teacher of Jainism

ca. 566–ca. 486BCE: Life of Prince Siddhartha Gautama (the Buddha)

4th–1st century BCE: Early Buddhist texts

5th–4th century BCE: The Sanskrit grammar of Panini

ca. 322–298BCE: Reign of Chandragupta Maurya

ca. 268–232BCE: Reign of Ashoka

3rd century BCE: Earliest strata of the *Ramayana* and the *Mahabharata*

3rd–2nd century BCE: The *Dharma Shastra* texts

2nd–1st century BCE: Early texts of the Hindu philosophical schools (*saddarsana sutra*)

1st century BCE: The early (Cankam) period of Tamil texts

1st–2nd century CE: The Kushana empire

ca. 78–101: Reign of Kaniskha as the Kushana emperor

1st century: Early Mahayana Buddhist texts

1st century: The *Kama Sutra* attributed to Vatsyayana

2nd century: The *Natya Shastra* on aesthetics, attributed to Bharata

ca. 50BCE–250CE: Satavahana dynasty dominant in the Deccan area

320–335: Reign of Chandra Gupta I, from the capital at Pataliputra

335–370: Reign of Samudra Gupta

375–415: Reign of Chandra Gupta II

415–454: Reign of Kumara Gupta

ca. 3rd–7th centuries: Bhasa, Kalidasa, and other early classical Sanskrit writers

ca. 540: End of the Gupta dynasty

606–647: Reign of Harsha of Kanauj

5th century: Classical Tamil compositions

6th–9th centuries: Pallava dynasty dominates Tamil Nadu, South India

630–668: Reign of Narasimha Verman of the Pallava dynasty

712: Arab conquest of Sind

757–973: Rashktrakuta dynasty dominates Karnataka, South India

ca. 760–1140: Pala dynasty dominates Bengal and Bihar, eastern India

ca. 8th century: Sankara, founder of the Advaita Vedanta philosophy

ca. 850–1279: Chola dynasty dominates South India

985–1014: Reign of Rajaraja Chola

1012–1044: Reign of Rajendra Chola

1012–1026: Mahmud of Ghazni's sack of Hindu "temple-cities"

1171–1206: Reign of Muhammed of Ghor

1192: Defeat of Rajput armies by Ghor at the second battle of Tarain

1206–1211: Reign of Qutb ud-Din Aibak, first ruler of the Delhi Sultanate

1206–1290: The Slave Dynasty of Delhi

1290–1320: The Khilji Dynasty of Delhi

1320–1413: The Tughlaq Dynasty of Delhi

1336–1565: Vijayanagar empire

1509–1529: Reign of Krishnadeva Raya of Vijayanagar

1451–1526: The Lodhi Dynasty of Delhi

1526–1707: The Great Mughal period

1526–1530: Reign of Babur

1530–1556: Reign of Humayun

1556–1605: Reign of Akbar

1605–1627: Reign of Jehangir

1628–1657: Reign of Shah Jehan

1658–1707: Reign of Aurangzeb

1674–1680: Reign of Shivaji, king of the Marathas

FURTHER READING

Basham, A.L. *The Wonder that was India: A survey of the history and culture of the Indian sub-continent before the coming of the Muslims.* London: Sidgwick & Jackson, 1967.

Brockington, Joseph L. *The Sanskrit Epics.* Leiden and Boston: E.J. Brill, 1998.

Buitenen, J.A.B. van. *Studies in Indian Literature and Philosophy.* (Edited by Ludo Rocher.) Delhi: American Institute of Indian Studies and Motilal Banarsidass Publishers, 1988.

Craven, Roy C. *Indian Art: A concise history.* New York: Thames and Hudson, 1997.

Dehejia, Harsha V. *The Flute and the Lotus: Romantic moments in Indian poetry & painting.* Ahmedabad, India: Mapin, 2002.

Dehejia, Vidya (editor). *The sensuous and the Sacred: Chola bronzes from South India.* York: American Federation of Arts; Seattle: University of Washington Press, 2002.

Eaton, Richard M. *Essays on Islam and Indian History.* New Delhi: Oxford University Press, 2002.

Flood, Gavin (editor). *The Blackwell Companion to Hinduism.* Oxford and Malden, Massachusetts: Blackwell Publishing, 2003.

Gaston, Anne-Marie. *Bharata natyam: from temple to theatre.* New Delhi: Manohar, 1996.

Harle, J.C. *The Art and Architecture of the Indian Subcontinent.* Harmondsworth, Middlesex, and New York: Penguin Books, 1986.

Hiltebeitel, Alf. *Rethinking India's Oral and Classical Epics: Draupadi among Rajputs, Muslims, and Dalits.* Chicago, Illinois: University of Chicago Press, 1999.

Huntington, Susan L. *The Art of Ancient India: Buddhist, Hindu, Jain.* New York: Weatherhill, 1985.

Keay, John. *India: A history.* London: HarperCollins, 2000.

Klostermaier, Klaus K. *Hinduism: A short history.* Oxford: Oneworld, 2000.

Kosambi, D.D. *The Culture and Civilisation of Ancient India in Historical Outline.* London: Routledge and Kegan Paul, 1965.

Krishna Chaitanya. *A History of Indian Painting.* New Delhi: Abhinav Publications, 1976.

Kulke, Hermann and Dietmar Rothermund. *A History of India.* London and New York: Routledge, 1990.

Lamotte, Etienne. *History of Indian Buddhism: From the origins to the Saka era.* Louvain-la-Neuve: Université Catholique de Louvain, Institut Orientaliste, 1988.

Lidova, Natalia. *Drama and Ritual of Early Hinduism.* Delhi: Motilal Banarsidass Publishers, 1994.

Mansingh, Surjit. *Historical Dictionary of India.* Lanham, Maryland: Scarecrow Press, 1996.

McLeod, W.H. *The Sikhs: History, Religion and Society.* New York: Columbia University Press, 1989.

Metcalf, Barbara Daly and Thomas R. Metcalf. *A Concise History of India.* Cambridge and New York: Cambridge University Press, 2001.

Nilakanta Sastri, K. A. *A History of South India from Prehistoric Times to the Fall of Vijayanagar.* Oxford and Madras: Oxford University Press, 1966.

Pesch, Ludwig. *The Illustrated Companion to South Indian Classical Music.* Oxford and Delhi: Oxford University Press, 1999.

Rahman, A. *History of Indian Science, Technology and Culture, AD1000–1800.* Oxford and New Delhi: Oxford University Press, 1999.

Renou, Louis. *The Civilization in Ancient India.* (Trans. Philip Spratt.) Calcutta: South Asia Books, 1997.

Robb, P.G. *A History of India.* Basingstoke: Palgrave, 2002.

Schimmel, Annemarie. *Islam in the Indian Subcontinent.* Leiden: E.J. Brill, 1980.

Schopen, Gregory. *Bones, Stones, and Buddhist Monks: Collected papers on the archaeology, epigraphy, and texts of monastic Buddhism in India.* Honolulu: University of Hawaii Press, 1997.

Sewell, Robert. *A Forgotten Empire (Vijayanagar): A contribution to the history of India.* New Delhi: Asian Educational Services, 1988.

Sharma, Arvind. *Hinduism and its Sense of History.* New Delhi and Oxford: Oxford University Press, 2003.

Sharma, V.K. *History of Jainism: with special reference to Mathura.* New Delhi: D.K. Printworld, 2002.

Smith, Vincent Arthur. *The Oxford History of India.* Oxford: Clarendon Press, 1964.

Srinivasiengar, C.N. *The History of Ancient Indian Mathematics.* Calcutta: World Press, 1967.

Stein, Burton. *A History of India.* Malden, Massachusetts: Blackwell Publishers, 1998.

Stone, Anthony P. *Hindu Astrology: Myths, symbols, and realities.* New Delhi: Select Books, 1981.

Taranatha. *History of Buddhism in India.* (Trans. L. Chimpa and A. Chattopadhyaya; edited by Debiprasad Chattopadhyaya.) Calcutta: Bagchi, 1970.

Thapar, Romila. *A History of India* (vol. 2). Baltimore, Penguin Books, 1965.

Vatsyayan, Kapila. *Traditional Indian Theatre: Multiple streams.* New Delhi: National Book Trust, India, 1980.

Wheeler, J. Talboys. *India of the Vedic Age: with reference to the* Mahabharata. Delhi: Cosmo, 1973.

INDEX

PICTURE CREDITS

The publisher would like to thank the following people, museums and photographic libraries for permission to reproduce their material. Every care has been taken to trace copyright holders. However, if we have omitted anyone we apologize and will, if informed, make corrections to any future edition.

Key:

AA	Art Archive, London
AKG	AKG-images, London
Axiom	Axiom Photographic Agency, London
BL	British Library, London
BM	British Museum, London
CC	Chris Caldicott
J-LN	Jean Louis Nou
V&A	Victoria and Albert Museum, London

1 V&A; **2** AKG-images/J-LN; **3** V&A; **6** Axiom/CC; **7** AKG/Nimatallah/National Museum of India, New Delhi; **9** Michael Holford, Loughton; **11** BL; **13** Axiom/CC; **14** AA/Dagli Orti (A)/National Museum, Karachi; **15** Dinodia, Mumbai/; **19** V&A; **20–21** A.F. Kersting, London; **23** AKG; **24** V&A; **25** Axiom/Ian Cumming; **26** Axiom/D. Shaw; **27** A.F. Kersting, London; **28** Axiom,/CC; **29** AKG/Gérard Degeorge; **30–31** SuperStock/AGE Fotostock; **32** AKG/J-LN; **33** AA/Dagli Orti (A)/Biblioteca Nazionale Maricana, Venice; **34** AKG/J-LN/Jagdish and Kamala Mitaal Museum, Hyderabad; **37 & 38** V&A; **40–41** Corbis/Galen Rowell; **42** Axiom/CC; **45** AKG/J-LN; **46 & 49** V&A; **50** AKG-/J-LN/Dogra Art Gallery, Jammu; **53** V&A; **54 & 56** BL; **57** AA/BL; **58** BM;

60 AA/Bodleian Library Oxford (Douce Or a1 f.21r); **61** AKG/J-LN; **63** V&A; **64** Dinodia, Mumbai; **65** AKG/J-LN/Government Museum, Madras; **67 & 68** BM; **71** V&A; **72** A.F. Kersting, London; **75** V&A; **77** AA; **78** V&A; **81** Axiom/CC; **82–83** Alamy/Eddie Gerald; **84** Dinodia, Mumbai; **86 & 87** V&A; **88** AKG/J-LN; **89** A.F. Kersting, London; **90–91** AKG/J-LN; **92** Axiom/Dinesh Khanna; **95, 96, 97 & 98** V&A; **100** AKG/J-LN; **101** AKG-images/Musée Guimet, Paris; **102** V&A; **104–105** Dinodia, Mumbai; **106** BM; **107** V&A; **108** BM; **111** V&A; **112–113** Axiom/CC; **114** V&A; **117** AKG/J-LN/Lucknow Museum; **118** AA/BL; **119** Science Museum, London; **121 & 122** V&A; **125** BL; **127** AA/BL; **128** A. F. Kersting; **131** Wellcome Library, London; **132** V&A; **134–135** Dinodia, Mumbai.